Chui Wan

*An Ancient Chinese
Golf-Like Game*

An analysis by

*Anthony Butler, David Hamilton
and John Moffett*

*Including a new translation of the Wan Jing
by Chuan Gao and Wuzong Zhou*

St Andrews 2017

Created for the Partick Press, St Andrews, Scotland
Design by George Bowie and cartography by Graeme Sandeman.
Every effort has been made to trace the originals of the Chinese images used.
Supported and printed by CreateSpace

ISBN 978-0-9510009-5-3

The Chui Wan Team:

ANTHONY BUTLER was born in London in 1936. After attending London University, he was later appointed to the permanent staff of the University of St Andrews to teach in both the chemistry department and medical school. In 1980 he met Joseph Needham of Cambridge University (author of the multivolume work *Science and Civilisation in China*) and became interested in the history of science and technology in China, publishing a number of studies in collaboration with Needham. He retired in 2001 and was appointed honorary professor.

DAVID HAMILTON is a retired Glasgow transplant surgeon. He studied immunology with Sir Peter Medawar and has published on the history of both surgery and golf. He served on the Heritage Committees of both the Royal and Ancient Golf Club and the United States Golf Association and lives in St Andrews.

JOHN MOFFETT graduated in Chinese at the University of Edinburgh, and lived in China for a number of years. As a fluent Chinese linguist, he is currently librarian of the Needham Research Institute in Cambridge.

CHUAN GAO was born in China, where she qualified as a medical doctor at the Medical School, Zhejiang University. She obtained her Ph.D. on health pyschology from Aberdeen University. She enjoys reading classical Chinese literature and visits China regularly.

WUZONG ZHOU was born in China. He obtained his B.Sc. degree from Fudan University and his Ph.D. from Cambridge. He moved to St Andrews in 1999 after living in Cambridge for 15 years. He is currently professor of chemistry at St Andrews University.

Table of Contents

❧

❧

Preface

Our attempt to understand the Chinese stick-and-ball game of *chui wan* played during the Song and Yuan dynasties and to assess its influence, if any, on the development of golf in Europe turned out to be a more complicated task than we first imagined. We have tried to make the story as simple as possible, but if matters are made too simple they become untrue. It is important to remember that Chinese civilisation is much older than that of the post-Classical civilisation of Europe. Dates that seem so early by European standards are not so when applied to Chinese society. That a sophisticated stick-and-ball game should have been played by the Chinese in 10-12th centuries should not surprise us. Assessing the possibility that what happened in China at that time influenced events in Europe is a difficult matter and involves the recounting of some Chinese history. We have tried to keep this to a minimum, but history is rarely simple. Part of the book is concerned with understanding how *chui wan* was played and this is much simpler.

∞

In matters of usage we have endeavoured to be consistent throughout the book. The romanised version of Chinese used is the *pin yin* system, general throughout mainland China. All *pin yin* terms are italicised, a commonly-used convention. If the *pin yin* version of a Chinese character is pronounced as if it were English, the sound is approximately that of the Chinese character. Unfortunately, this does not work too well for the name of the game with which this book is concerned. The two character name (捶丸) given to it by the Chinese means 'hit ball' and the *pin yin* version is *chui wan*. The first of these is pronounced 'chuwee'. We tried hard to find a more easily pronounced English name but were unsuccessful. The direct translation ('hit ball') is not very elegant and 'strike ball' leaves the reader mystified. So we are stuck with *chui wan*. The Chinese game of *wei qi* is successfully rendered in English as simply Go as translated from Japanese, but calling *chui wan* simply Hit does not really work. We have not combined the two, as is commonly done, to give *chuiwan*, nor have we hyphenated the two, as has been done elsewhere, to given *chui-wan*. Keeping them separate is closer to the Chinese original. For named persons we have kept the traditional Chinese pattern of putting the family name first, then the given names. Where the person concerned has adopted the Western pattern of putting the family name second, we have done so.

For dates we have used the convention of CE (Common Era) and BCE (Before the Common Era) rather than AD and BC as the latter are not relevant to a non-Christian civilisation. The actual numbers are the same.

This book covers a range of topics: translation from classical Chinese (very different from modern Chinese), Chinese philosophy and history, art and social customs as well as the history and rules of modern golf. We have tried to ensure accuracy by reference to reliable authorities but they do not always agree. We hope that any differences do not substantially affect the general thesis of the book.

જી

Painting based on a mural from the
Shuishan Temple in Shanxi Province.
Courtesy of ancientgolf.missionhillschina.com

Chapter One: Introduction

Anthony Butler and John Moffett

Golf is a game played throughout the world and great players have emerged from many countries. It is not surprising that, in recent time, China has joined the golf-playing nations of the world and there are now many talented Chinese players on the international scene. Along with this blossoming talent has come evidence that in former times (Song, Yuan and Ming Dynasties 960 – 1500 CE) Chinese people played a stick-and-ball game, rather similar to modern golf, called *chui wan* ('hit ball'). A number of articles have appeared in the press over the years claiming that this game is related, in some way, to modern golf. In 1991 there was a significant review of the evidence by Ling Hongling, then professor of Physical Education at Lanzhou University.[1] Ling concluded that playing *chui wan* started in the Song Dynasty (960 – 1279 CE). As evidence he reports that in the Dongxuan Records by Wei Tai of the Song Dynasty there is an account of a county magistrate's instructions to his daughter on how to dig holes in the ground and to drive a ball into them.[2]

The earliest visual evidence for the playing of a stick-and-ball game in ancient China comes from a mural on the wall the Shuishan Temple in Shanxi Province (facing).[3] It dates from the Yuan Dynasty (1260 – 1368 CE) and shows people with sticks but it is not entirely clear what they are doing. In the painting there are four men, two in red and two in blue. The men in blue are carrying clubs and those in red appear to be hitting balls into a hole in the ground. There is no indication that the game being played was called *chui wan* but it is most certainly a stick-and-ball game, played on a compact playing area, similar, as we shall see, to *chui wan*.

Additional visual information about the nature and style of *chui wan* play comes from two Ming Dynasty (1368 – 1644 CE) paintings still extant and in excellent condition. The first (below) is entitled *Emperor Xuanzong of the Ming Is Playing* and shows Emperor Zhu Zhanji (1426 – 1435 CE) playing a stick-and-ball game in the grounds of the Summer Palace.[4] The holes are marked with flags in a clearly delineated playing area. A variety of club appears to be available and the Emperor looks as if he is choosing between two of them for his next stroke on a permanent playing area. An even more precise and sophisticated painting of a game of *chui wan* is seen in part of a handsome scroll by the Ming painter Du Jin (active 1465-1509 CE) entitled *Ladies in the Inner Court Palace* (Figure 3). The original hangs in the Shanghai Museum.[5] A full interpretation of this painting requires some understanding of artistic movements in Ming Dynasty China.

Painting entitled
*Emperor Xuanzong
of the Ming is Playing* held in
the Palace Museum, Beijing

Scroll painting entitled *Ladies of the Inner
Court Palace* held at the Shanghai Museum

In the mid-Ming Dynasty there was a literary movement called *fu gu* ('return to antiquity') that was concerned with the revival of texts from earlier dynasties. It also led to a movement among painters to portray contemporary scenes peopled with figures from the past. Du Jin was one such painter and the handscroll shows ladies, probably concubines from the court, in Ming dress participating in activities of a previous age within a palace garden. The activities portrayed are gossiping, playing with a child, playing kickball (*cu ju*) and, most significantly, playing *chui wan*. The scene depicted must be from a former age as, by the Ming Dynasty, women had their feet bound at quite an early age and would have been incapable of playing *chui wan*, let alone *cu ju*. So, for Du Jin's immediate audience the scene was clearly historical.

∞

In the *chui wan* section of the scroll there are five figures. Two of them are carrying clubs and appear to be functioning like modern caddies. The fact that they are both carrying more than one club might suggest that there were clubs of different designs available to the players but a closer examination of the painting shows that they are all the same design. However, this might be because Du Jin did not know enough about the game to illustrate the types of clubs used by players. During the Ming Dynasty, when he was painting, the playing of *chui wan* was dying out. When this painting was put on display at the Victoria and Albert

Museum in London in 2013, as part of a comprehensive exhibition of Chinese painting, it caused much interest in golfing circles in Britain, as it challenged the notion that golf had been developed in Scotland during the fifteenth century and then exported to China in the twentieth. A headline in *The Times* of London read: 'Ming Dynasty ladies of leisure tee up battle over the birth of golf'. Were Chinese people playing golf long before it was known anywhere in Europe?

Although the painting by Du Jin is both arresting and captivating, it tells us nothing about the aims and aspirations of the players. It is possible to imagine stick-and-ball games in which play is very different from the game of modern golf. This matter will be discussed in more detail in Chapter 8. Fortunately the rule book for playing *chui wan* (the *Wan Jing*, 'ball manual') written by Ning Zhi Lao Ren, with additional comments by an unknown author, still exists. Printed by block printing, it was first published in 1282 CE and by others thereafter. Our copy is held in Cambridge University Library. It will be discussed more fully later. It consists of 32 rules of play and some of them are quite lengthy and give a different view of the game. When Ling wrote his review in 1991 the *Wan Jing* had not been fully translated into modern Chinese or into English.

Some parts had been extracted and used by scholars to illustrate the importance of etiquette in the Chinese game. Several of the rules quoted indicate strongly the value associated with behaving like a gentleman while playing. In this regard it is similar to modern golf (at its best) but before we can confidently assert that *chui wan* is the same as, or at least a precursor of, modern golf a complete translation of the *Wan Jing* is needed in the expectation that it would disclose exactly how the game was played. After all, good manners during play is not unique to golf; players of bowls are equally well-behaved. Our aim has been to provide a full, scholarly translation of the *Wan Jing* into English to allow us and our readers to compare *chui wan* with modern golf and decide upon the relationship between them. A full explanation of some of the technical terms used has not been attempted, notably in the description of making implements in Rule 18.

ⅎ

In the course of the production of our translation, which proved more difficult than we had anticipated, it was pointed out to us that one translation had already been published. It was made by the distinguished sport historians, the late Max Howell and his wife Lingyu Xie.[6] It was published in Australia as an e-book under the title *China, the Birthplace of Golf?* We found this translation very helpful in a number of places but, in others, we preferred a rather different rendering of the text. More significantly, our aim has been rather different from that of Howell and Xie. The *Wan Jing* consists of a set of rules (in classical Chinese) interspersed with a commentary written some hundred or so years later. In Howell and Xie's translation these two are combined to give a composite rule. We have kept the two separate and in the complete translation is given in the final Chapter of this book;

the commentary is given in parentheses after the original rule. This arrangement will allow other scholars to assess the accuracy of our translation and to offer alternatives leading to a clearer understanding of the original. This rather wordy translation will be of greater interest to those with knowledge of Chinese than to the general reader. For the benefit of the latter, we have provided, in Chapter 2, an abridged set of rules with just enough detail to capture the essence of each rule. From this abridged set of rules it should be possible to see how the game of *chui wan* was played. For the translation we were fortunate enough to interest two Chinese-born scholars Wuzong Zhou and Chuan Gao, who, although they have both lived in Britain for many years, have a profound and abiding love of the Chinese language and culture.

80

In Chapter 3 we offer our best understanding of how the game was played. We think it is fairly certain that there were other local versions of the game (discussed in Chapter 2) and that the *Wan Jing* was an attempt by one man to bring some order out of the confusion. We hope our version comes somewhere near a correct understanding of the game. We have played our version of *chui wan* on a hilly putting course and found it entertaining .

Whether *chui wan* is a form of golf, the precursor of modern golf or an entirely distinct game with an ethos all of its own is something we discuss in Chapter 4. That the etiquette of *chui wan* owes much to The *Analects* of Confucius is a matter we explore in Chapter 5.

References

1. Ling Hongling (1991)'Verification of the fact that golf originated from chuiwan' *Bulletin of the Australian Society for Sports History*, 14, 12-22.

2. Wei Tai, *Dongxuan Records*, volume 12, from *First Collection of Books*.

3. Reproduced in *Guangshengsi*, Cambridge University Library.

4. Painted by Shang Xi, a Ming Dynasty court painter (Collection of the Palace Museum, Beijing).

5. Painted by Du Jin (Shanghai Museum), 31919.

6. Lingyu Xie and Max Howell, *China: the Birthplace of Golf?* (Palmer Higgs, Victoria 2012).

Chapter Two:
Abridged rules and guidance
for playing *chui wan*

Anthony Butler

This account is taken from the translation of the *Wan Jing* by Chuan Gao and Wuzong Zhou given in full in Chapter 10.

Rule 1: Traditional play
All players must obey the regulations and anyone not doing so should be expelled from the game. To decide who goes first, throw the ball and the player with the longest throw wins. Once play has started, you cannot change the club selected. If the ball is moved by a player or by the wind it counts as a stroke. Players should never gloat or show anger.

Rule 2: Correct play and guidance
You can make a mound of earth for the first shot. If you cheat you will soon be found out.

Emperor Xuanzong c1430, of the Ming dynasty, the world's first identified stick-and-ball game player: National Palace Museum, Taipei.

Rule 3: Time of play

Select a day that is sunny, but not hot, for a game. Choose a time to play that does not interfere with your work.

Rule 4: The playing area

The playing area should have a varied terrain, with depressions and raised areas. When playing downhill, be gentle. If play is uphill it is easier to hole the ball. Be particularly careful if the ground is flat. The clubs for long shots should be kept in a bag, but clubs for short shots from a crouching position are kept in a basket. Having prepared all the relevant equipment, you cannot lose.

Rule 5: The condition of the ground

The playing area may be hard or soft, dry or wet. When the ground is hard, players should reduce the power of their stroke but increase it when the ground is soft. Play according to the state of the ground, wet or dry. In doing so you are more likely to win.

Rule 6: Establishing the playing area

Select a site to play, remove rubble and mark the area, about one foot square, for the first stroke (the 'base'). There should be no practice swings on the base. At the same time, no-one should approach the base in case they tinker with it. Moving the ball after it has landed should be punished by missing two turns. This rule should prevent fraudulent behaviour. [We think the first part of Rule 6 means that, because the courses were often rough, a player is allowed to clear a small area to enable him to make a proper first shot.]

Rule 7: Selecting fellow players

Select fellow players who are respectful, peaceful and serene: they will admire the skill of others. Unworthy players use low tricks in order to gain an advantage. Competitions between gentlemen are always about skill. A gentleman is always cautious in his choice of friends.

Rule 8: Playing etiquette

Dig hole(s) and insert flag(s). The players should play strictly according to the rules. Players with literary talent and honesty are acceptable because they play in a relaxed, cheerful and elegant manner. Do not allow yourself to become exhausted.

Rule 9: The order of play

The player who makes the first stroke chooses a place to set a base but the second stroke is taken where-ever the ball lands. The order of play is decided by throwing a ball towards the hole; the closeness of the ball to the hole when it comes to rest decides who has first choice for the initial strike. The second strike is from where-ever the ball lands. Anyone repositioning the ball after the first stroke is despicable.

Rule 10: Technical aspects

Players may hit the ball from either a standing or squatting position, but different clubs should be used. When some distance from the hole, do not squat to make a stroke. When making a shot, hold the club tightly in a palm-to-palm position.

Rule 11: Marking the position of the ball

Mark the position of where the ball has landed. If anyone moves it accidently, it should be replaced in its original position and he loses a stroke. If the original position has not been marked, then the ball should not be moved back. If two balls end up very close together and there is also an obstruction, both balls may be moved to a better position. If a player's ball hits another person he may replay the shot if he wishes and the person hit loses a playing token.

Rule 12: Prize money

Everyone should contribute to the winning prize; the wealthy should be generous and the poor should be careful. Good players often win but those with little skill may lose all their money.

Rule 13: Scale of competition

When there are many players, possibly up to ten, they should play as two teams, but three or five players can play as individuals. For team matches, the winning team is the one winning most holes, as in matches between single players. When there are three or five individual players, only one can win. Do not participate in more than three games in one day.

Rule 14: Playing tokens

A player's performance is rewarded with the playing tokens. Holing the ball in one stroke gets three tokens, in two strokes two tokens and if three strokes are required, only one token. For team games, the winner is the first team to acquire 20 tokens in a big match, 15 in a medium-sized match and just 10 in a small match. Once a player has holed his ball, there is no more play at that hole. If all players in a game take more than three shots to hole the ball, no playing tokens are awarded.

Rule 15: The wind

When the wind blows a ball into a hole it does not count as a winning stroke, if the others have played. However, if the wind blows the ball into the hole while it is being played, this does count as the winning stroke. Using the wind to win is an excellent strategy; it takes advantage of good fortune.

Rule 16: The lie of the ball

It should be possible, if skilled, to play a ball even when it is in an unfavourable position. Worthy players have confidence and do not fear to play, while unworthy players are fearful. Winners are usually gentle people and are polite to other players.

Rule 17: Manufacture of balls and clubs

Balls for playing *chui wan* should be carefully measured spheres of wood. Clubs should have a length appropriate for the player's height. Makers of clubs and balls should select the best wood available. Success in *chui wan* does not depend on strength but on knowledge of the ground conditions.

Rule 18: Implements

Use well-made clubs and practise your strokes. You will be able to hit your ball into the hole whenever you play.

Rule 19: Good equipment

Good equipment is necessary to win when playing *chui wan*.

Rule 20: Distances

The maximum distance between the hole and the playing base should be no more than a 100 strides (about 40 metres) while the minimum should be more than 25 strides. Long initial shots are tiring. Also, with long shots it is more difficult to hole the ball. If you are a weak player, leave the long shots to those who are stronger, but no-one should try long initial shots too often. Equally do not use too many short initial shots.

Rule 21: Behaviour during play

Players should not teach others how best to play a particular course. You must not prevent, in any way, others from scoring points. Hitting another player's ball causes a penalty and you are disqualified if you obstruct another player. Collusion with a friend to change the course of play should result in banishment.

Rule 22: Examining the terrain

Do not glance around as you hit the ball, for concentration aids good play. If you carefully consider the terrain you will win. If you rely solely on strength only luck will bring you victory.

Rule 23: Etiquette during play

People will judge you by your behaviour. Talking little and acting promptly are both signs of good behaviour and are characteristic of a gentleman.

Rule 24: Mental attitude

A player should be focussed but not obsessed with the desire to win. No tactic is more shameful than moving the ball by hand after it has landed.

Rule 25: Wisdom

With a good technique a player can always find a way to win and to do so quietly. Players with noble minds abhor underhand ways of playing but lesser players sometimes use them.

Rule 26: Winning tactics

To hole a ball when there are others nearby can sometimes be difficult. Be daring. Sometimes a powerful shot is needed; other times a clever but gentle shot will suffice. Occasionally the ball goes into the hole unexpectedly. At other times, try as hard as you can and even cheat, your shots fail. Consider everything carefully before you make a stroke and you will win all the time. There is an old saying that a small difference at the beginning results in a thousand mile difference at the end.

Rule 27: Motivation

People play well only when they are motivated. Study the motivation of others and you will see what they are trying to do. Motivation decides who wins or loses.

Rule 28: Advice on winning

High and long shots require powerful strokes. A player should focus on winning. Honourable players are not indifferent to who wins or loses.

Rule 29: State of mind

Nothing is more important than getting players in the right state of mind. Observe other players' expressions, body language and tone of voice. If your opponents display anxiety, use this to help you to win. You should stay calm while they start to panic. Victory then is certain. However, success is ensured only if you remain cautious from start to finish.

Rule 30: Harmony

Honourable people have nothing to prove and play in a pleasant way. Harmony without conformity is the ideal. To win by the use of servility and flattery is not honourable.

Rule 31: Good manners
Some players always wait for late-comers but late-comers should be seen as self-centred persons. Frivolous behaviour should be recognised as tawdry and malicious actions as bad manners. People who are lame, blind, hunch-backed or deaf should not play *chui wan*. Equally, scoundrels are unwelcome. There has never been merging of the classes in *chui wan* matches. Worthy players do not show conceit or haughtiness after a run of victories nor annoyance after repeated failures.

Rule 32: Knowing your fellow players
A player's mind should be at peace and his calm temperament should reflect a relaxed body. His aspirations and intentions will be obvious from his appearance. If players are restless, show disrespect and become indignant, their anger will show. Honourable people remain calm and peaceful. When the result of the game has been determined the competition ends.

&

Chapter Three:
How to play *chui wan*

Anthony Butler

It is not easy to deduce from the 32 Rules contained in the *Wan Jing* how *chui wan* was played. The same would be true if you tried to see how modern golf was played by reading the current Rules of Golf. The Rules and the *Wan Jing* are both more concerned with dealing with infringements, cheating (or, rather, preventing it) and behaviour during play than with the actual procedure of play. Also, there appear to have been many different ways of playing *chui wan* (Chapter 2) and this makes establishment of a playing procedure even more challenging. We have done our best to devise a game, to be played on a pitch and putt course today, that incorporates as many of the 32 Rules as possible. Where no guidance is given, or when the guidance is obscure, we have made what we hope are informed guesses and hope that what emerges is identical with one version of the game played in Song, Yuan and Ming dynasty China. The scoring system, but not stroke play, differs according to the number of players (Rule 13) so we have given separate accounts of a game of, say, three players playing as individuals, and a match between two teams, each of three players.

The male pronoun is used throughout as, when the rules were first formulated during the Song or Yuan dynasties, it is unlikely that women played. The painting by Du Jin, showing court ladies at play, is a piece of Ming dynasty artistic licence. *Chui wan* appears not to have been a pursuit of only the leisured classes as Rule 3 warns players to choose an appropriate time for play that does not interfere with work.

Chui wan is essentially a gambling game and part of the enjoyment would be lost if there are no stakes to play for. But Rule 12 tells players to keep the stakes low to avoid penury and we earnestly advise aspiring players to follow this advice. The playing tokens can be any counters and should be carried by one of the players, unless you are lucky enough to have the luxury of a caddy.

A number of rules (eg Rule 10) suggest that you should have a range of different clubs but no account of how they differ is given. Aerial shots are mentioned (Rule 10) and so, as well as a putter, something akin to an iron is required. However, on a normal pitch and putt course a putter alone would suffice. In view of the competitive nature of the game, all players should have the same clubs.

Setting up the course

Chose an area of uneven grassland (Rule 4) and dig a hole or holes that can be marked with flags (Rule 8). Play on a modern pitch and putt course is even better. No fixed number of holes is required. In fact, you can keep playing the same hole over and over again until, as will be explained in the scoring section, the game is won by one player. Divide the distance (which should be about 100 strides or 40 metres) between the start (ie the tee) and the hole into three equal sections. The first third is the 'playing area' and a ball may be hit for the first time from anywhere within the playing area. The aim is to get the ball into the hole in three shots or fewer. The distance should be such that a good player, hitting his ball from that part of the playing base nearest the hole, has a chance of getting a hole in one. The number of strokes taken to hole the ball affects the scoring.

Playing the game

It is important to select fellow players who are appropriate. They should be 'respectful, peaceful and serene' (Rule 7). Players with literary talent are particularly acceptable (Rule 8). An appropriate contribution from each player is put into a kitty to provide the prize money (Rule 12). To decide the order of choice for the first shot, but not the actual order of play, throw a ball towards the first hole (Rule 9). The player whose ball lands nearest to the hole has first choice. If he elects to play from the back of the playing area (ie farthest from the hole) he goes first; if he chooses the front of the playing area (nearest to the hole) he goes third. If he selects the mid-position he goes second. The player with second choice may select one of the two positions left by the first player and the third player has the remaining position. The player selecting the back position has the most difficult challenge but has the first strike. The mid-base player goes second and the front-base player goes third. That order of play is maintained until one player gets his ball into the hole. Tokens are awarded (see next section) and a second hole is played. For the first shot only, players are allowed (Rule 2) to place the ball on a mound of earth, rather like a modern tee.

Ester Paolocci, Emily Bradeen,
Anna Rauter, Charlotte Müller and
Janet Butler, lady students of
St Andrews playing *chui wan*.

Photograph by Sam Taylor

The order of choice (selection of position within the playing area) amongst players for restarting and playing the hole for a second time is unclear. It could be the same as that for the first time but that might seem to give an unfair advantage to the player with first choice. However, further consideration shows that this would not necessarily be the case. If he always chose the easiest position (that nearest the hole) he would always play last and skilled play on the part of his opponents might rob him of the chance of holing the ball first. Probably the order of choice (which must be distinguished from the order of play) should remain the same throughout a match. In Rule 20 players are warned against choosing the back-base position too often in any one match.

Strokes should be made from either an upright position or while squatting (Rule 10). Players today might find the latter rather uncomfortable and it is difficult to see what advantage it would give.

Scoring system

Once one player has holed his ball play ceases and that player is given playing tokens, the number depending upon the number of strokes taken: three tokens for a hole in one, two tokens if two strokes are taken and only one token for three strokes. Holes are played, or the same hole replayed, until one player has accumulated 10 tokens (Rule 14). That finishes the match and he then takes the prize money. If a ball has not been holed within three strokes, play is discontinued and a new hole started.

Scoring in team games

It is more difficult to discern the scoring system for team games than when individuals are involved as the *Wan Jing* is unclear. The simplest scheme seems to be to play each hole in pairs and award playing tokens according to the same principle as that for individuals. The winning team is the first to amass, as a team, 20 playing tokens or any other number that seems appropriate.

Penalties

When things go wrong, or a player is caught cheating, penalties are applied. According to Rule 1 any player ignoring the regulations should 'be punished without forgiveness'. This sounds rather harsh and should be applied only to persistent offenders. The penalties range from losing one or two turns or shots. to losing the game or even being thrown out of the event.

Players must not practise swings on the playing base (Rule 6).

An opponent's ball must not be interefered with (Rule 21)

Players must not hover near the hole in case they tinker with it (Rule 6).

Moving a ball by hand after it has landed is strictly forbidden and punished by missing two turns (Rules 6 and 9).

Players should not rush forward or move about impatiently (Rule 8).

If a player accidently moves a ball it should be re-placed to its original position and the player loses a turn (Rule 11).

If a player's shot hits a person he may replay it if he wishes to do so (Rule 11).

Players should not teach others how to play best on a particular course (Rule 21).

Hitting another player's ball or obstructing another player results in a penalty of losing a turn or banishment (Rule 21).

Behaviour while playing

Much is made throughout the *Wan Jing* of behaving like a gentleman. This includes not cheating, not talking all the time, not losing one's temper when things go wrong and not gloating when you win. Rule 16 indicates that the winner should be gentle and polite to others. In summary, behaviour should conform to the Confucian ethic. You are advised to choose your fellow players with care and to avoid those who are unworthy. Much has been made of the special etiquette of *chui wan* but it is not unlike that of most noncontact sports which includes, of course, modern golf. The insistence on gentlemanly behaviour is partly the influence of Confucianism in all aspects of human behaviour within Chinese society but is also required because of the strong element of gambling in the game.

Miscellaneous matters

Some of the rules of *chui wan* concern situations that seem unlikely, like massive obstructions and unruly behaviour. They can be studied in the complete translation of the *Wan Jing*, given in Chapter 10, but are unlikely to be of interest to anyone trying the game today. In conclusion it should be emphasised that a close reading of the complete set of rules given in Rule 10 suggests that each group of friends had their own set of rules for playing *chui wan*. This is not unlike the early days of Scottish golf. The *Wan Jing* is an attempt to bring some order to the confusion and there are inconsistences within the *Wan Jing*. This means that there are inconsistences between the game we have described and some of the rules given in the *Wan Jing*. Some readers the *Wan Jing* may disagree with our interpretation and prefer anther version of the game. We do not claim that ours is the only version, or even the best version, of the game. But it is a version that contains many of the basic elements of the game played in Song and Yuan China. One major difficulty we have had is deciding how many holes there were in a *chui wan* 'course'. We feel, on balance, that generally there was only one hole and that it was used repeatedly until one player won. But we should not exclude the possibility that in some version of the game there were several holes. The number of holes was not fixed and it did not matter, as the collecting of playing tokens, rather than the number of holes won, decided the winner. One major inconsistency needs special comment. The two paintings shown in Chapter 1 show a playing area completely different from that described in the *Wan Jing*, as does the Autumn Banquet scene (see over). In the paintings the playing area is much more like that of a modern putting green. It is possible that the Chinese played a game very like modern putting, as well as all the variants of *chui wan* hinted at in the *Wan Jing*.

Ming Dynasty Scroll *The Autumn Banquet*
shows noble play in a confined area.

Chapter Four:
Chui wan – the game, and a comparison with modern golf

David Hamilton

The debate on the origins of modern golf has been a long and continuing one.[1] Importantly, it has been realised that the word 'golf' has been used too loosely historically and a helpful clarification in the debate has been to instead use 'stick-and-ball game' for the group of sports which resemble modern golf. This caution prevents prejudging any game before examining its relationship with golf.

Before looking at the claims of *chui wan* to be a precursor of modern golf, the first step is to define the characteristics of our own familiar game of golf. Importantly, early Scottish stick-and ball games in Scotland had two forms, both called 'golf'. One form, like modern golf, was played on the east coast by well-off players using expensive balls and clubs, and, first noted in the 1400s, it can be called 'long' golf.[2] The simpler 'short' golf was played throughout Scotland in the town streets and churchyards with simple home-made equipment; it resembled some of the European stick-and-ball games of the time but the rules are unknown.

The players of 'long' golf sought out the extensive linksland found near many of the east coast towns. These well-off players regularly returned there for the sporting challenge offered by miles of fine turf kept short by the tramp of feet and cropped by grazing animals, notably sheep. These golfing links were playable in both winter and summer. The extensive, varied area chosen for play was split up into a number of successive 'holes', some short and some long, with the hole length varying between 100 yards to 500 yards. The number of holes was later standardised at a total of 18.[3] Play on the links was made more difficult by the presence of 'hazards', notably sandy bunkers and whin bushes, which, instead of being a drawback, were a part of the golfing challenge, and the quality of these hazards was a feature at these favoured venues. In playing long golf, the special feather-filled ball flew far when hit towards a small hole in the ground. A variety of expensive clubs were in use, starting with a long first shot, followed by more delicate strokes when nearing the hole. In match-play, then and now, usually two players play against each other. The person taking the fewer strokes wins the hole, and, restarting at the next hole, the match continues when one player obtains an unassailable lead. Some features which are found in other stick-and-ball games are absent from golf, notably any race to the hole, or regular interference with the opponent's ball.

The Venues

How does this Chinese game *chui wan* compare with the long game of golf?[4] In spite of the difficulties in understanding the arcane and often obscure ancient text in *Wan Jing*, a fairly clear idea can be obtained as to how it was played. A small playing area in a 'peaceful park or garden', convenient for the players is chosen for play, rather than regularly returning to gather at a favourite, fixed course. Play is sometimes between two players, but much in the rules suggests that there were important competitive *chui wan* gatherings, involving quite large teams, and that on the day, the players were accompanied by supporters. The social side is mentioned and the players drink and eat together.

Importantly, it seems that the playing area was only one 'hole' which was played repeatedly, rather than embarking on a succession of holes, as in long Scottish golf.[5] Play is not on grass, but over rough grassless earth, and the ball can be 'dead' i.e. unplayable, at times. No water hazards are mentioned. These compact playing areas make for awkward play, and 'hindrances' behind the starting point are mentioned in Rule 6 which can restrict the backswing. Beyond the hole, the ball may hit further hindrances, such as walls (Rule 4) and rebound back. The ball can lodge in trees (Rule 8), calling for tricky second shots. The playing area seems crowded at times with the players and spectators, but no animals are present, unlike the situation on the early Scottish links. There is no mention of a lost ball, again suggesting that the playing area is limited and that play is watched closely by spectators. The length of the hole, given in Rule 20, varies from 40 yards down to 1 yard, with 20 yards the more usual length. Holing out in one shot is mentioned in a number of the Rules, as if quite common, confirming that short holes were much in use.

A very short form of the game, like putting, may have been popular, as favoured by the Emperor Xuanzong, who is seen in the illustration in Chapter 1 starting play on a small flat area with five holes and flags. The format of play on any particular day may have varied according to preference or depended on the number of players who turn up.[6]

Playing the game

The form of play ranges from 'singles' – one player against another – to more competitive gatherings at which up to six, eight or ten may play after splitting up into a complex team format. The players have a set number of 'tokens' – counting chips – in hand, collected from the 'ticket office' at big events (Rule 8). These are won and lost depending on the strokes taken at each hole, gaining three tokens for a hole in one, two for holing in two and one token for taking three shots. In the complex team game, the winner is declared when the team accumulates 20 tokens. The players in the singles matches start with five tokens each, and lose the game when these are gone. But added to this, Rule 14 mysteriously says that the first to hole out wins the hole, and then the other players cease play. The tokens won cannot be carried over to the next day's play, when play starts over again. Betting is added to the game, namely gaining and loosing the prize money contributed, according to wealth, by all involved. Money seems to change hands during the day's play, since Rule 12 mentions that players can run out of money after each game, during the main event.

The complex play on the day (Rule 3) seems to involve three components, like tennis, namely starting with playing the single hole up to five or seven times, which makes up a game or set, and then three sets go towards an overall match.[7] The format of play on the 5-hole putting green, used by the Emperor at play is not described, but must allow a decent match of reasonable length.

On the day of play, Rule 8 shows that 'hole(s) are dug' and coloured flag(s) inserted and since the Chinese language does not use plurals, this leaves the matter undecided. Rule 21 mandates that a new playing area is created for each day's play; this is in fairness to new arrivals who had no experience of the first day's playing area. No dimensions of the holes in the ground created is given, but those in the image of the Emperor at play are quite small. However, on the main playing area, the size of the hole might be quite large, since Rule 15 refers to the regular occurrence of the ball being blown into the hole by wind.

The first shot is played from a 'tee' described in Rule 6 made by clearing debris from the starting area and adding enough earth to give a small, one foot square area called the 'base'. The earth cannot then be disturbed in any way thereafter, including compacting it with a club, and the base is then used by all the players for their first shot. For the second shot, the ball is played where it lies. If it lands close to an opponent's ball, Rule 11 says that the ball should be marked carefully with a stick placed one inch away. Breaking the complex rules leads to many sanctions and there are three levels of penalty – loss of tokens, loss of strokes and even expulsion from the competition. These infringements and the penalties are given in Chapter 3; no method of refereeing is mentioned.

Balls and clubs

A wooden ball is used, as described in Rule 17 made from wood galls – the dense 'burrs' or 'burl' growths on trees. Players have their favourite size, which is also suited to their clubs, and size of the ball is checked by measurement with metal rings. The best balls are those with surface pores. Coloured balls (mentioned in Rules 2 and 24) are used in the large team format to prevent the wrong ball being played. Balls said to be from the *chui wan* era are seen in the illustration, and are similar in size to golf balls.[9]

A variety of expensive clubs are used, suggesting a rich man's game, but there is a limit to carrying more than ten. The 17 varieties of club are described in Rules 17 and 18 and include the multipurpose *cuan* variety, also the *pu* clubs suited to long shots and the thin-headed *shao* clubs also used for short or aerial shots. These *shao* clubs are useful for lofting the ball over obstructions, and in evading a 'stymie' near the hole. One-handed shots are mentioned, and a squatting position, using an 'eagle-beaked' club, is used for short shots;[10] both these unusual swings appear in the illustrations of *chui wan*.[11] The clubs, made by skilled artisans, have a wooden head,

Clubs held in the Shanghai Sports Museum are described as *chui wan* club replicas based on decayed earlier finds. Wooden balls are also exhibited.

with added leather either covering the head or inserted into it. No iron-headed clubs are mentioned. In the illustration of the Emperor at play he is shown holding two clubs, one of which is eagle-beaked, selected from a collection of about 25 clubs under the care of servants. The clubs shown held by the court ladies in Chapter 1 are the thinner-head variety. Bamboo could be used for making the shaft and Rule 19 describes how it is best obtained in winter. The shaft is joined by glue to the head, and the clubs, made by skilled artisans, have a grip for the player's hands. The head of the club could be damaged by a poor shot, but there is no mention of the shaft breaking during play, suggesting that powerful shots were seldom used. The clubs are carried in a basket or leather sack, with servants acting as caddies. There is a collection of what are described as surviving *chui wan* clubs at the China Sports Museum in Shanghai, and, as shown, they include the eagle-beaked variety and also some with thin heads.[12]

The psychology of winning and the importance of winning is emphasised, as is the danger of self-confidence. There are many comparisons with military strategy. The writer of *Wan Jing* and the editor are both at pains to emphasise their own skill and experience, and that players would benefit from the wisdom offered in the book. However, the prohibition in Rule 31 against playing with disabled people is hardly high-minded. Overall, both the author and editor give a perhaps over-sophisticated account of this fairly simple game The equipment recommended seems elaborate, and the advice that the best equipment necessarily gives the best play seems naive.

Another feature of the book is the constant emphasis by both the author and editor on the etiquette of the game and the need for gentlemanly behaviour. The repeated warnings about cheating suggest that deceit was common, particularly when strangers or neophytes were involved in the *chui wan* gatherings. Players could be ejected from the event if their offences were serious. Historians have suggested that looking at the rules for sport reflect the attitudes of society at the time, and that as society changed, the rules steadily introduced into sport revealed new civilised behaviour, including a reduction in physical and verbal violence, and fairness in outcome.[13] The European rules are usually dated to the 1600s, and thereafter spread outwards from the increasingly sophisticated etiquette of the royal courts.[14] The *chui wan* rules show an earlier attempt to civilise a game, and perhaps a nation, in which disorderly conduct was common. These attitudes are discussed further in Chapter 5.

A Comparison

Chui wan and Scottish long golf have some similarities. A small ball is directed at a hole with a variety of clubs. But *chui wan*, even in its longest form, shows important differences from modern golf. *Chui wan* was played in different forms, with a variable length of playing area on any convenient rough ground, rather than on the lengthy, fixed, coastal grassland courses always favoured for the long Scottish game. In its longest form, *chui wan* was played to a single hole, usually under 40 yards away, and this hole was played to repeatedly by all the players. There could be obstructions like stones, walls and trees. A small wooden ball was used and hit with towards a hole with a variety of clubs. A short, putting, variant of *chui wan*, as shown in the painting of the Emperor, involved play on numerous short holes

Any open area would do for *chui wan* play rather than return to fixed, favourite venues. We can conclude that the games are not identical, and there is no literary evidence that the Chinese game did influence events in Scotland. In addition, it should be noted that the Chinese game is closer to the Scottish long game of golf than any of the European stick-and-ball games of the Middle Ages. This suggests that *chui wan* in its entirety was not transmitted from China via Europe to Scotland.

	Chui wan	*'Long' Scottish Golf*
Ball	Small wooden	Feather-filled
Clubs	Various wooden	Various wooden, plus one 'bunker' iron
Hole(s)	Mostly single, short	Many, long
Scoring	By shots taken Token system	By shots taken
Venue	Any urban space	East coast links
Hazards	Walls, stones, trees	Bunkers, whins

References

1. Geert and Sara Nijs *Games for Kings and Commoners: Colf, Crosse, Golf, Mail*, Bourgogne 2011.

2. David Hamilton *Golf – Scotland's Game*, Kilmacolm 1998.

3. Peter Lewis *Why Are There Eighteen Holes? St Andrews and the Evolution of Golf Courses*, St Andrews 2016.

4. Chinese-language publications on *chui wan*, as yet un-translated, include Nin Zhi Lao Ren 'Wan Jing' in Haipeng Zhag (ed) *Xue Jin Tao Yuan*, Yang Zhou 2008, Jiashi Wang 'From the editions of *Wan Jing* to study the development of the ancient batting ball' *Journal of Xi'an Institute of Physical Education* 22 (2005); 61-63 and Bingguo Liu and Shengping Zhang *Chui Wan: Golf in Ancient China*, Shanghai 2005. The few relevant English language publications are listed in Chapter 1; see also ref 6 below and Gui Yan, Zheng Tianju, Han Liebao, 'The study of chui wan, a golf-like game in the Song, Yuan and Ming dynasties of Ancient China' *Journal of Sports History*, 39 (2012), 283-297.

5. It is nowhere stated clearly that only one hole was used, but it is the assumption, throughout particularly Rule 4.

6. Rule 1 mentions that two forms of the game, *Wo-jiao* and *Hui-er* had evolved in the previous century, differing in the clubs used and the length of the playing area.

7. This five or seven hole format for a set shows that the single hole was not played out and then back again to the start, since an even number would be played. The large number of players on the hole would also have prevented this.

9. A personal collection of 1,000 *chui wan* balls is described by Wu Linqui 'Did Yuan Dynasty Mongols bring golf game into Europe?' *Golfika*, 1 August 2010, 40-44; only a minority are of wood.

10. The 'eagle-beaked' club is remarkably similar to the club used for short shots in the European game of crosse (see Chapter 6).

11. One-arm shots are depicted on Ming Chinese pottery (see absolutechinatours.com) and squatting European colf players are famously depicted in Simon Bening's 16th century *Book of Hours*; see Nijs (ref 1) p47.

12. These clubs and balls were displayed at the China Golf Association's 'Origins of Golf' exhibition in Beijing in 2006; see ancientgolf.missionhillschina.com.

13. For the rise of gentlemanly behaviour in sport, usually dated to the 17th century Europe, see Norbert Elias and Eric Dunning *Quest for Excitement: Sport and Leisure in the Civilising Process*, Dublin 1978.

14. The first Olympic Games in Greece had rules governing the events, and Europe's first sporting rules (for jousting) appeared in Spain in the 1300s.

論語卷之一　　朱熹集註

學而第一　此為書之首篇。故所記多務本之意。乃入道之門。積德之基。學者之先務也。凡十六章。

子曰。學而時習之。不亦說乎。

說悅同。○學之為言效也。人性皆善。而覺有先後。後覺者必效先覺之所為。乃可以明善而復其初也。習。鳥數飛也。學之不已。如鳥數飛也。說。喜意也。既學而又時時習之。則所學者熟。而中心喜說。其進自不能已矣。程子曰。習。重習也。時復思繹。浹洽於中。則說也。又曰。學者將以行之也。時習之。則所學者在我。故說。謝氏曰。時習者。無時而不習。坐如尸。坐時習也。立如齊。立時習也。

有朋自遠方來。不亦樂乎。

樂音洛。○朋。同類也。自遠方來。則近者可...有

The *Analects* of Confucius, circa 4th Century
BCE, influenced the text of *Wan Jing*.

Chapter Five:
Confucianism and the rules of *chui wan*

Anthony Butler and John Moffett

The game of *chui wan* was devised, according to the researches of Ling Hongling,[1] during the Song Dynasty (960-1279 CE) as this is when the first references to the game appear. The only set of formalised rules known to date is the *Wan Jing*, which has been translated for this book (Chapter 10). The preface of the *Wan Jing* indicates that it was written in 1282 CE, during the Mongol Yuan Dynasty, just after the final conquest of the Southern Song Dynasty. These rules go far beyond the technicalities of how to play the game and include a set of demanding rules of etiquette for those playing. That these rules were written down reflects aspects of the profound social and economic changes that were characteristic of this period. The movement during the Southern Song of the imperial and government elite and other wealthy families to the Jiangnan region of the lower Yangzi, and the rapid expansion of the economy, led to the growth of towns and cities and an increase in those with education and leisure time. The emphasis on etiquette in the *Wan Jing* not only reflects these changes but also the philosophical and political beliefs that lay at the foundation of Chinese society.

The Doctrines

Three philosophical systems rivalled one another in the Song period: Daoism, Buddhism and Confucianism, known as the 'Three Doctrines'. Daoism (sometimes

One of the many non-authenticated likenesses of Confucius.

romanised as Taoism) is a system of beliefs indigenous to China and based on the teachings of the sage Laozi. It emphasised living in harmony with the *dao* (the way) that underlies all things. It came to embrace an eclectic mix of philosophy, folk religion, ritual magic, meditation and monastic practice that catered to both the philosophical leanings of the elite as well as the everyday needs of the common people. Buddhism came to China from India and is based on the teachings of the Indian prince Siddhatta Gotama (563-483 BCE). It is a set of beliefs and practices which, it is claimed, released the individual from the endless suffering and cycles of rebirth inherent in human existence. After its arrival in China in the early centuries of the Christian era, it spread rapidly under the patronage of some Emperors, with many large and wealthy monasteries across China.

Most significant for us, however, is the third doctrine: Confucianism. Born out of the rituals and values of the age-old ancestral cult of the early Chinese cultures of the Yellow River Valley, Confucianism is less a religion than a system of moral and social precepts based on family hierarchy, encapsulated by Confucius (or Master Kong) in his *Analects*.[2] The name Confucius was coined by Jesuits who made the first translation of The *Analects* into Latin.[3]

Confucius is thought to have lived from 551 to 479 BCE, but the first biography of Confucius was not written until five centuries later and contains an abundance of fantastic stories and so he must remain, unless further scholarship and new archaeological evidence produces some hard facts, a rather mysterious figure. But the wisdom of his utterances is as relevant today as it ever was. The perception of Confucius in the West has ranged from the patron saint of the Enlightenment to

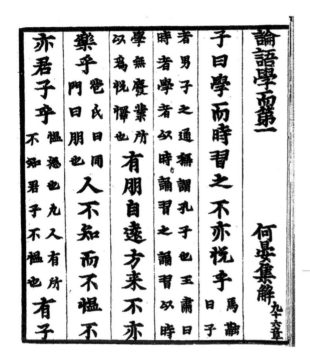

Lunyu jijie (Collected Commentaries on the Analects), 1922, Hanfenlou, Shanghai, translation of the Japanese edition of CE 1364.

the comic character uttering trite remarks, generally of a saucy character, in pidgin English. This comic characterisation is deeply insulting to a person of great stature and of whom the Chinese are very proud. In recent years Confucius has given his name to institutes all over the world promoting Chinese culture.

The *Analects* consists of about 500 pithy aphorisms organised into twenty Rules, thought to have been written down by his disciples and their followers in the decades after his death.[4] Confucius seems to have been a genial fellow, remembered by his disciples as much for his jokes and his expressions of self–doubt as for his profundities. He changed his mind, there are inconsistences in his thought and he displayed what would be seen now as unacceptable prejudices. In the centuries following his death a number of other texts became associated with him and the ritualists who emphasised his fundamental belief in the role of ritual in maintaining a stable society and the transformative nature of education and learning on the individual and society. These texts came to be known as the 'Four Books and Five Classics'.

Through 400 years of the Han Dynasty (206 BCE - 220CE), these texts and the exegetical tradition that built up around them became the dominant influence on elite culture and government. The behavioural norms enshrined in them defined what it was to be a cultured 'gentleman'. Knowing the texts by heart also became the foundation of learning and the qualification for advancement in the civil bureaucracy, eventually through the examination system, which became fully developed by the Song Dynasty.

Gentlemanly behaviour

Thus, the *Analects* and the precepts it embodied had become the foundation of the mental and moral make-up of all well-educated 'gentlemen' and those aspiring to be seen as such by the end of the Song. In such a culture, which valued and revered the written word above all else, composing the text of the *Wan Jing*, writing down the rules of the game of *chui wan*, as we have them in the *Wan Jing*, was a conscious attempt to elevate the game to an activity worthy of a 'gentleman'. So, it is no surprise to find that the moral precepts of Confucianism are reflected in the written rules of the game and even to echo passages of the *Analects*. Below we provide a few examples.

For the next section we have used the translation into English of the *Analects* by Raymond Dawson[5] and published in 1993. Before seeking to show links between some of the sayings in the *Analects* and the rules for playing *chui wan*, it is necessary to explain the usage and meaning of certain words in Dawson's translation.

The Chinese character *zi* is translated as 'master'. *Kongzi* is given as Master Kong but should not be seen as indicating teacher or philosopher.

The term *junzi* occurs frequently in the *Analects* and has been translated as 'gentleman', although in other translations 'the noble man' and the 'superior man' have been used. It means a man who has embraced the Confucian way of life and is an ethical term rather than one indicating social class.

The 'small man' (*xiaoren*) is the opposite of a gentleman.

The good is 'above' and the demeaning is 'below'.

The term 'antiquity' is used with great veneration as Confucius thought there was a 'golden age' in the distant past when men behaved in an exemplary manner both publically and privately.

The 'humane man' is another term for a gentleman.

With that introduction it is now possible to see substantial similarities between some of guidance offered in the *Analects* and the rules given for the conduct of a game of *chui wan*. In some instances the similarities are real but slight; in other cases they are substantial. For this section we have used only the original statement of the Rule, not the commentary added at a later date.

Rule 1   ... ignoring the traditional style of play should be punished without forgiveness.

Analect 7.1   Being fond of truth, I am an admirer of antiquity.

Rule 7   **Therefore, you should make friends with the gentlemen and stay far away from the villains.**

Analect 16.4   It is beneficial to make friends with the upright, to make friends with the sincere, and to make friends with those who have heard many things.

Rule 8   Players with literary talent and honesty are acceptable ...

Analect 12.24   The gentleman collects friends through culture and through his friends supports humaneness.

Rule 8   The party should play as a group and share the entertainment derived. Everyone must play strictly by the rules and do what they should do. Rushing forward and running about impatiently, shouting and clamouring, make these people unworthy players and they should not be approached.

Analect 3.7   There is nothing which gentlemen compete over. But they go up, bowing to each other; and when they come down, they have a drink. So even in their competition with each other, they are gentlemen.

Rule 16   Worthy people have confidence and do not fear to play but unworthy people have no confidence and are fearful.

Analect 12.4   The gentleman is neither worried nor afraid.

Rule 22   Although players who play with their strength may sometimes win the game, they win by luck.

Analect 6.19   The fact that a man lives is due to uprightness. If he spends his life without it, he is lucky to survive.

Rule 23   Talking little, acting promptly and fulfilling what you say are all signs of good behaviour.

Analect 3.24   The gentleman wishes to be slow in speech but prompt in action.

Rule 26   Occasionally the player does not expect to hole the ball but achieves it. In other cases, the player desperately wishes to hole but cannot achieve it.

Analect 9.22   There are times ... when plants shoot but do not flower, and when they flower, do not produce fruit.

Rule 29.   If you are winning from an early stage, you must not become
                 conceited.Conceit will definitely lead to failure.

Analect 13.26   The gentleman is dignified but not arrogant.

Rule 30.   Some players act servilely with over-praising in order to win.
                 Honourable people do not appreciate this.

Analect 7.16   Riches and honour acquired by unrighteous means are to me like
                 the floating clouds.

Rule 30.   Worthy people have nothing to prove. Develop a good relationship
                 but maintain individual players' personalities

Analect 23.23   The gentleman, although he behaves in a conciliatory manner, does
                 not make his views coincide with those of others.

Rule 30.   Being servile and ingratiate themselves. These people are flatteres.

Analect 5.25   Clever words, a plausible appearance and excessive courtesy [are]
                 shameful.

Rule 32   Your mind likes to be peaceful. Your aspirations and interests like
                 to be appropriate. Your facial expressions should show respect to
                 others.

Analect 6.2   Surely it is all right if one adopts easy going practices for the sake
                 of dealings with other people, provided that one occupies a basic
                 position which commands respect.

The similarities between some of rules of *chui wan* concerned with the etiquette of
play and the *Analects* reflect the pervasive influence of the teachings of Confucius
many centuries after his death. In addition to the particularised similarities shown
above, there is the general ethos of both the Rules and the *Analects*. The Confucian
ethical system was the prerogative of the upper classes, which included civil servants
and scholars, but did not reach out to merchants and the artisans who tilled the
soil. It is explicitly stated in Rule 8 that for a game of *chui wan* there are acceptable
people ('those with literary talent') and, by implication, unacceptable people. Rule
31 makes it clear that *chui wan* was an exclusive game ('From the earliest time there
has not been mingling of the classes'). The prejudice in Confucian times against
those who were not gentlemen parallels the dislike of 'trade' in Victorian Britain.
The Rules of *chui wan* also shows a lack of compassion by specifically banning the
'lame, blind, hunch-backed or deaf from playing'. There is nothing exactly parallel

to this in the *Analects* but Confucius showed an equally heartless attitude to women. In Analect 17.23 he says 'Only women and small men seem difficult to look after. If you keep them close, they become insubordinate; but if you keep them at a distance, they become resentful.' He offers no advice or remedy.

Thus, these rules, their appeal to the *Analects*, and their presentation in textual form implies that playing *chui wan* was an activity worthy of a Confucian gentleman, or an aspiring one, governed by the same rules of conduct as poetry, painting, the appreciation of antiques and scholarly conversation. Etiquette is what one would expect from a gentleman playing *chui wan* and the Rules merely remind him to maintain standards of conduct at all times.

References

1. Ling Hongling (1991) 'Verification of the fact that golf originated from chuiwan' *Bulletin of the Australian Society of Sports History 14*, 12-22.

2. A C Graham, *Disputes of the Tao: Philosophy and Philosophical Argument in Ancient China*, 1989, Open Court, La Salle, Illinois.

3. L Jensen, *Manufacturing Confucianism*, 1998, Duke University Press, Durham.

4. D Hall & R T Ames, *Thinking through Confucius*, 1987, State University of New York Press, Albany.

5. R Dawson, *The Analects*, 2000, Oxford University Press, Oxford.

Boy with Colf Club (1603)
Attributed to Adriaen van der Linde
(Dutch artist, 1560-1609)

Chapter Six:
Stick-and-ball games in Europe

David Hamilton

The records of many nations from earliest time mention games in which balls were hit with sticks.[1] In looking for the origins of modern golf, however, we can narrow down the possibilities after excluding adversarial team matches like hockey and mounted sports like polo. This leaves a group of European games, found mainly in North West Europe in the Low Countries, France and Belgium, but which are, surprisingly, not found in Germany, Spain, or Portugal. These can be looked at closely for any linkage to Scottish golf. These games often showed local variants, and merged with each other, but four are fairly well described. Persisting for centuries, the European games were richly illustrated, unlike the situation in Scotland. The features of the modern game of golf are given in chapter 4, and, briefly stated, are that it is, and was, a 'long' game played with a set of clubs to a series of holes over miles of suitable turf. Hazards are encountered, and at each hole the player who takes the least strokes is the winner.

The four European games are characterised by the distinctive clubs used.

Colf and Kolf

The earliest known European stick-and-ball game is colf (or colven) described in the Low Countries (i.e. Holland and Belgium) from 1261.[2] As shown in the painting opposite, it was played with a wooden-shafted club with a distinctive metal head (of

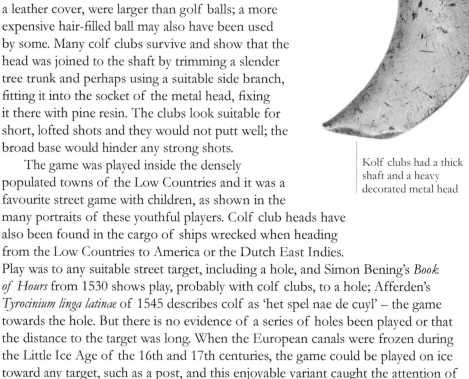

lead or iron) which had a triangular cross-section and a broad base.

The balls used, made of wood with or without a leather cover, were larger than golf balls; a more expensive hair-filled ball may also have been used by some. Many colf clubs survive and show that the head was joined to the shaft by trimming a slender tree trunk and perhaps using a suitable side branch, fitting it into the socket of the metal head, fixing it there with pine resin. The clubs look suitable for short, lofted shots and they would not putt well; the broad base would hinder any strong shots.

The game was played inside the densely populated towns of the Low Countries and it was a favourite street game with children, as shown in the

Kolf clubs had a thick shaft and a heavy decorated metal head

many portraits of these youthful players. Colf club heads have also been found in the cargo of ships wrecked when heading from the Low Countries to America or the Dutch East Indies. Play was to any suitable street target, including a hole, and Simon Bening's *Book of Hours* from 1530 shows play, probably with colf clubs, to a hole; Afferden's *Tyrocinium linga latinae* of 1545 describes colf as 'het spel nae de cuyl' – the game towards the hole. But there is no evidence of a series of holes been played or that the distance to the target was long. When the European canals were frozen during the Little Ice Age of the 16th and 17th centuries, the game could be played on ice toward any target, such as a post, and this enjoyable variant caught the attention of artists. No rules for playing colf have survived and hence the detailed style of play is unknown, nor were there any favourite, fixed locations for play. The format was probably variable and agreed in informal ways among those gathered to play.

Colf died out by the 1700s. As the towns grew in size this hazardous street game was specifically discouraged by town regulations. The agricultural land outside to towns was unsuitable for play and the coastal landforms, though similar to Scottish links, were far from the inland towns, and were not used for sport. The earlier claim that there was a long cross-country variant of the game, with a series of holes, has been revealed as a 'hoax'.[3]

Instead, in the Netherlands a sophisticated game emerged called kolf, played by well-off players on a short formal court. The club now was thick-shafted with a heavy curved metal head which propelled a large wooden ball toward a post on the court about 20 yards away. The rules of kolf were first regularised in 1769, and the game still persists in a small way today.

Crosse and mail

A less common game existed in the Low Countries from 1332, called 'crosse' (or choule or chole) which still has a small and enthusiastic following.[4] Played in uncultivated fields the club used had (and has) a heavy square head with one slightly lofted side to use for long shots. Turning the club through 90°, the hooked beak can be used for short shots near the target or to play out of ruts. It is unique in using elliptical balls, originally of wood, but now made of plastic. From 1885, the game gained an official organisation with written rules, and it survives, played by farmers, near the Franco-Belgian border. Players approach a two foot high metal target about 20 yards away and the first player is allowed three shots to reach and hit it. If not, the opponent can then 'de-chole', as in croquet, and hit the opponent's ball away from the target, before their own three attempts. Once the hole is completed, a series of holes follow.

A 20th century crosse player hitting the elliptical ball with the flat side of the club. Woodcut 'Les Crosseurs' by Marius Carion in Achille Delattre *Histories de nos corons*, 1939

The game of Jeu de mail emerged in Italy and moved thence to Mediterranean France in the 15th century, and became popular with the aristocracy. The first written rules for play emerged in 1637 at Utrecht. The game was played along a formal court of about 100 yards in length (as at Pall Mall in London), or along longer alleys towards a ring or post as target. The heavy two-headed club, not unlike a croquet stick, has one flat end and the other is lofted for the shorter shots. In sme variants, a second smal iron club was used for the final 'shooting the passe' shot. The cross-country 'chicane' variant played along narrow paths persisted in France until 1930.

Jeu de Mail was played with a heavy, dou-ble-headed club and a large ball. (From Joseph Lauthier *Nouvelles règles pour le jeu de mail*, Paris 1717.

Shinty

The Irish team game camanachd – called 'hockey without rules' – is mentioned in 12th century documents and it probably reached the north-west of Scotland quite early. It persists as the team game of shinty in the north of Scotland, played with a simple curved stick and wooden ball. Early Irish accounts of the game describe a short individual variant of the game played to a hole. Shinty may have encouraged the 'short' game of golf in Scotland's early Lowland towns.

The features of what is known of these games can be summarised thus:

	Colf	Kolf	Mail	Crosse	Long Golf
First noted	1261	1769	15th Century	1332	1400s
Target	Varied	Post	Post or ring	Broad Post	Hole
Club(s)	Single, metal head	Single metal head	Two - one double-head	Single double-head	A set
Ball	Wood	Wood	Wood	Elliptical wood	Feather-filled
Hole Length	Varied	22 yards	c100 yds	c100 yds	100-500 yds
Series of Holes	No	No	No	Yes	Yes
Location	Varied	Formal indoor court	Outdoor court	Rough ground	Linksland
First Rules	Unknown	1769	1637	1885	1743

References

1. Robert W Henderson *Ball, Bat and Bishop: The Origin of Ball Games* University of Illinois Press, 2001 and Michael Flannery and Richard Leech *Golf Through the Ages,* Golf Links Press 2004.

2. Confusingly, the game of 'colf' was also called 'kolf' in some sources.

3. Michael Flannery *Golf International* (2009); 3-32.

4. Geert Nijs and Sara Nijs *Choule: the Non-Royal but Most Ancient Game of Crosse,* Bourgogne 2008.

Chapter Seven:
The early Scottish rules of golf - a comparison with *chui wan*

David Hamilton

The format of Scottish 'long' golf, the game played with the featherie ball and expensive clubs, would be in place from the 1500s, and be similar to the modern game. They would have a code of well known rules shared among the scattered groups of players, one so well known that there was no need for them to be written down. The need for a written code came in 1744 when the Edinburgh golfers (later the Honourable Company of Edinburgh Golfers) organised an open tournament at Leith and, concerned that there might be disputes, and with many lawyers in the group, the captain wrote down the generally-accepted rules for play. These rules included one 'local' rule for play on their Links. Very similar rules emerged in other golfing societies, notably at St Andrews ten years later, suggesting that there was a long-standing agreed code for the game in Scotland. Later, the St Andrews golfers took the name Royal and Ancient Golf Club, and with the popularity of the Old Course, the St Andrews rules became nationally recognised. Now, coordinated with the United States Golf Association, it is an international code.

Lees *A Golf Match* St Andrews circa 1847
Courtesy of the National Galleries of Scotland

These two sets of rules - for *chui wan* and long golf - can be looked at and compared. The Leith rules are reproduced using the original spelling, capitalisation and punctuation:

Rule 1: You must Tee your Ball within a Club's length of the Hole.

As play proceeded to the next hole, there being six at Leith, the first shot at the new hole was played from a spot close to where the previous hole finished. There is no comparable rule in *chui wan*, suggesting again that only one hole was played repeatedly, with the players returning each time to the starting point where the special 'base' had been prepared.

Rule 2: Your Tee must be upon the Ground.

This puzzling rule does suggest that instead of sand for a tee, some Scottish golfers tried erecting a complicated teeing area, similar to *chui wan* 'base', but this complexity was discouraged.

Rule 3: You are not to change the Ball which you Strike off the Tee.

A featherie ball might perform poorly, or could be damaged, but the players could not substitute it during the playing of a hole. The robust wooden ball used in *chui wan* would not be damaged easily, and this mishap is not mentioned.

Rule 4: You are not to remove, Stones, Bones or any Break Club, for the sake of playing your Ball, Except upon the fair Green & that only within a Club's length of your Ball.

Evidently on Leith Links a fair amount of debris was encountered and this could not be removed, even though it might damage a club. *Chui wan* had a similar rule, and stones were particularly mentioned as a nuisance. However, at Leith, there was a smoother area around the hole – the 'fair green', later the simply 'the green' - which assisted skilled putting. Obstructions there could be removed. There is no equivalent area round the green in *chui wan*, though spectators were asked not to pass within five feet of the hole, to prevent any foul play.

Rule 5: If your Ball comes among Watter [water] or any wattery filth [cow dung], you are at liberty to take out your Ball & bringing it behind the hazard and Teeing it you may play it with any Club and allow your Adversary a Stroke for so getting out your Ball.

Leith Links could have areas of 'casual water' but also the problem of dung dropped by animals, notably the semi-liquid nuisance from cows. The *chui wan* rules have no suggestion that animals or their products were a problem on the short course used. The Scottish rule assumes that singles matchplay was the usual game, and the player was penalised one stroke if requiring to 'lift and drop'.

Rule 6: If your Balls be found any where touching one another, You are to lift the first Ball, till you play the last.

There is a comparable rule in *chui wan* which allows the ball to be lifted at any time after making a mark one inch distant from the ball. This was a prudent move if the opponent or his supporters were likely to interfere with the player's ball.

Rule 7: At Holling [putting], you are to play your Ball honestly for the Hole, and, not to play upon your Adversary's Ball not lying in your way to the Hole.

There is a similar rule in *chui wan* when play was near the hole.

Rule 8: If you shou'd lose your Ball, by it's being taken up, or any other way, you are to go back to the Spot where you struck last, & drop another Ball, And allow your adversary a Stroke for the misfortune.

At Leith Links, the ball might be picked up by other users of the Links or by animals, notably dogs. In the *chui wan* rules there is no mention of a lost or stolen ball. This again suggests repeated play over one hole, and since spectators ringed the compact area used and followed the balls, lost balls were unlikely. Cheating by kicking the opponent's ball away is mentioned in the Chinese rules however, and punished by loss of strokes, with the player's ball replaced.

Rule 9: No man at Holling [putting] his Ball, is to be allowed, to mark his way to the Hole with his Club, or anything else.

Chui wan has a similar rule.

Rule 10: If a Ball be stopp'd by any person, Horse, Dog, or any thing else, The Ball so stop'd must be play'd, where it lyes.

Leith Links seemed crowded with non-golfers and animals who might be hit by the ball. In *chui wan*, if spectators halt the ball, it also had to be played as it lay. However if these were known to be supporters of the opposing player, then that player was penalised.

Rule 11: If you draw your Club in order to Strike & proceed so far in the Stroke as to be bringing down your Club; If then, your Club shall break, in any way, it is to be Accounted a Stroke.

The powerful swing needed in Scottish 'long' golf could break the elegant long-nosed clubs, and if this happened after the downswing starts, the stroke counted.

In *chui wan*, the expensive clubs seen in the illustrations seem fragile, but there is mention only of damage to the head with a careless shot, and no allowance for such damage.

Rule 12: He, whose Ball lyes farthest from the Hole is obliged to play first.

The same rule applies in *chui wan*.

Rule 13: Neither Trench, Ditch or Dyke [embankment], made for the Preservation of the Links, nor the Scholar's Holes or the Soldier's Lines, shall be accounted a Hazard; But the Ball is to be taken out Teed and play'd with any Iron Club.

Leith Links had been improved by drainage, and this unnatural, man-made system was not counted as one of the local 'hazards'. This suggests that other hazards existed, and other sources, notably the poem *The Goff* of 1743, describes bunkers at two holes on Links. This rule also shows that there was also a group of short holes for school children's play.

∽

Overall, in comparing the rules, the *chui wan* code is more detailed, even prolix, and its rules repeatedly had to deal with matters of etiquette, and penalties for cheating or foul play. Missing from the Leith rules was any mention of cheating, or exhortation to the players to behave like gentlemen. Otherwise many of the incidents requiring a ruling are likely to occur in any game in which a ball is directed towards a hole in the ground. Though separated by 500 years, these codes for the two stick-and-ball games show considerable similarities.

	Leith Rules	Chui Wan
Ball played as it lies	Yes	Yes
Remove obstructions	No, except on the 'fair green'	No
Hazards	No relief, except from drains	No relief
Lost ball	Penalty	Not mentioned
Broken club	No relief, if breaks after downswing	Not mentioned
Change ball in play	Not allowed	Not mentioned
Lift and mark the ball	If touching another ball	At any time
Penalties for cheating	Not mentioned	Numerous
Ball hits spectator	No penalty	Penalty if supporter
Scoring	Simple match-play assumed	Complex token system
Etiquette	Not mentioned	Many suggestions

嘉禾周履靖校正

金陵荊山書林梓

承式章第一

經丸之制全式為上破式次之達式出之一種

式先習家風後學體面折旋中矩周旋中

人利不嘖得雋不遜若喜怒見面利口傷人

不與相讓采索窩　讓人先拋毬見得采者

不與相讓　手中無攛者筭輸　一筭無應

木窩忘窩攛戒筭

Chapter Eight:
Did information about *chui wan* reach Europe?

Anthony Butler and John Moffett

Although there are many differences (see Chapter 4), some features of *chui wan* are so similar to those of modern golf that it is inevitable that there is speculation about a connection between the two. Did information about the Chinese game reach Europe, capture the interest of Europeans, particularly people living in The Netherlands and Scotland, and lead to the playing there of stick-and-ball games? It is necessary to establish that, firstly, there were, in the 12th and 13th centuries, channels of communication between the two cultures and, secondly, that information about *chui wan* did actually travel to Europe in this way. The search for evidence of the latter is made easier if strong evidence of suitable channels of communication has been established.

Playing *chui wan* appears to have first flowered in China during the Song Dynasty (960-1279 CE), one of the golden ages in China's history.[1] Although most famous for the flowering of the arts such as poetry and painting, many technological innovations, of which China is equally proud, occurred during the Song or became fully developed at that time. Such was the confidence of the Song Chinese that they had little interest in other civilisations. The name given by the Chinese for their country *Zhong Guo* (The Central Kingdom) is indicative of this attitude. Other

---

Wan Jing written in 1282 quoted and commented on an earlier code of play for *chui wan*.

The fabled Silk Road, a trade route carrying far
more than silk from China to the Mediterranean
for several thousand years.

countries in Asia looked towards the Central Kingdom; the Chinese reflected upon
their superiority. However, this did not stop the Chinese trading with other nations.
They had wonderful things to trade – principally tea, silk, porcelain, metallic objects
and medicinal rhubarb – and China required materials (principally spices, perfumes,
plant products for medical purposes and some metals) from other countries. The
great trade route to the West, the Silk Road, stretching from western China (modern
Gansu Province) through the kingdoms of central Asia to Iran and, eventually,
to the ports of the Mediterranean had functioned for over a thousand years but
became increasingly difficult during the 13th century because of encroaching desert,
and by the late Ming it had closed.[2] However, even in the Road's heyday, Chinese
merchants did not travel the whole length of the Road. Instead the goods were sold
on from one merchant to another through the kingdoms of central Asia and it was
probably Arab merchants who finally delivered the goods to the borders of Europe.
There is some evidence that, along the eastern part of the Silk Road, the main body
of traders were Sogdians, a group of people about whom very little is known. They
were part of the Iranian cultural sphere with Samarkand (in present day Uzbekistan)
as their capital city. A small number of letters in Sogdian were discovered by the
great Central Asian explorer Aurel Stein in his exploration of the Silk Road.[3] They
have now been translated[4] and are concerned mainly with matters of trade. Two
relevant facts emerge: firstly, there was a regular postal service along the Silk Road
and, secondly, the quantities of goods carried by the traders were small. The latter
suggests that the traders were small operators, eking out only a modest living by

trading, not the educated, cultured class of person who played, or was remotely interested in, *chui wan*. Even if some of the Chinese merchants who brought goods to the start of the Silk Road, but no further, had been early players of *chui wan*, the transport of precious goods to the West does not provide a likely route for *chui wan* to make the same journey.

An historical detail is consistent with the view expressed above.[5] In the ninth century trading activities along the Silk Road were concentrated in the Western Market of Chang'an (now Xi'an), the first city of the Road. Men, women, Chinese and foreigners crowded into a tight space to exchange news and to barter. However, officials above 5th rank, the sort of people who would have played *chui wan*, were not allowed to mingle in the market with commoners, the sort of person who might have ventured along the Silk Road.

Denizens of the classical world knew of China, they called it Cathay, and its advanced civilisation but knew little about it. Little changed during the first millennium although a certain amount of trade occurred. Even if Sogdian traders had carried information about *chui wan* westward that information would have to have passed on, yet again, to Middle Eastern Arab traders who, as true sons of Islam, should have eschewed the game of *chui wan* as gambling was strictly prohibited in the Qu'ran. The Prophet describes it as an abomination.[6] The possibility of Silk Road traders carrying a copy of the *Wan Jing*, as suggested by Ling,[7] is unlikely; they might have spoken a little Chinese but it is unlikely they would have been able to read it.

By Sea

The opening of sea routes for trade to replace the Silk Road made little difference. The notion that Chinese fleets made epic sea voyages to Australia and South America[8] has now been discredited by scholars.[9] Chinese ships traded extensively within Southeast Asia and visited ports in India and, possibly, the east coast of Africa (there were African slaves in China) but that was all. There, the cargo was unloaded and taken further by other ships but getting to Europe by sea was, at that time, impossible. To all intents and purpose, there was no direct contact between Song China and Europe. To be a little more precise: there is no evidence that Chinese people who might have a knowledge of *chui wan*, be they travellers, merchants or diplomats, ever reached Europe. At this period in history, information about *chui wan* stayed firmly within the Central Kingdom. Had the Chinese ever ventured, for diplomatic reasons, to Europe, the reverse journey was made by Europeans a century or two later, they might have taken *chui wan* with them but there is no evidence that they ever made the journey. There was a mission to the West in 8th century CE but it went no further than Iran. Scholars of the Song Dynasty did write about foreign countries[10] but their information was always second hand and, inevitably, contained many errors and exaggerations. It is also doubtful if information about a genteel stick-and-ball would have aroused much interest in Europe at that time when sport was synonymous with hunting, deer hunting, falconry and archery. The Greek interest in what we would now call field sports did not exist; however, they had a hockey-like game, one not featuring in the Olympics.

Rather than through direct trading link, there is a possibility that knowledge of *chui wan* could have come to Europe by diffusion of ideas through the Arab world. This appears to be the case with gunpowder, another Chinese invention. Joseph Needham, the great historian of all things technological in China, held tenaciously to the idea of diffusion of ideas and inventions to the West from China. As an example, he traced in great detail the journey of the formula of gunpowder through the Arab world to the West during the 12th and 13th centuries.[11] Likewise, printing (both block printing and printing with moveable type) may have made the same journey,[12] although this is less certain. Islam did not, at that time, permit the printing of the Qu'ran and so the value of printing in Arab society was much less than in the Buddhist culture of China where duplication of the Scriptures was considered a matter of great virtue. However, even he admits to a word of caution. He made the reasonable assumption that the longer the time elapsing between the appearance of an invention in China and its appearance in the West, the more likely it is that they were independently invented. The first printed formula for the gunpowder used in warfare appeared in China in 1044 CE and by the 13th century it was known in Europe. This is a relatively short elapse by the standards of the day. If *chui wan* was first played in the early Song, then it was 400 years before golf appeared in Europe, making diffusion difficult to credit.

A possible channel of communication opened after the Mongol conquest of China, following the Song Dynasty (around 1200 CE).[13] Originally the Mongols were a nomadic people living on the grasslands to the north of China. Life there was hard; it bred a tough and warlike race who were superb horsemen. They developed military power by perfecting the use of powerful archery skills from horseback. In a story as remarkable as any in human history, the Mongols embarked, under the leadership of Temujin later to become Chinggis Khan (sometimes written as Genghis Khan) to conquer neighbouring states. Their tactics involved jaw-dropping brutality but cities that surrendered without a struggle were treated with a measure of tolerance and, although many were enslaved, others were allowed to live a life, in some aspects at least, unchanged from that before being conquered. Providing tribute was paid, the conquered peoples were left alone. In this way, the Mongols built an empire that stretched from the east coast of China to the borders of Europe and included parts of Russia. The Mongol conquest of China started in 1211 CE with the gradual submission of North China but before the South was brought under Mongol domination, over 60 years had passed. The Mongol military operation in China was led first by Chinggis Khan.[14] He became Great Khan of the whole empire and entrusted the further conquest of China to his son Ögedei who died of alcoholism in 1241 CE and the final settlement was made by his son Qubilai Khan (1215-1294 CE). Qubilai Khan eventually became

Chinggis Khan, leader of the Mongols, established the largest empire the world has ever known and included China.

The Mongol Empire 1294

0   3000 km

Great Khan with his summer court at Shang Du (Coleridge's Xanadu) in Mongolia, some 100 miles north of Beijing. For cultural links the Mongol Empire provided a single empire that spanned the divide between China and the borders of Europe. Anyone chosing to do so could make that journey from China to Europe without leaving the Mongol empire[15].

Mongol Traders

The Mongols were great traders and Chinese goods found their way to Europe during the Yuan Dynasty. Under Mongol rule many new roads were built in China to facilitate the movement of goods. Merchants associations (known as *ortoq*) were established to allow for the insurance of goods being traded and staging post on the road were built where merchants could obtain fodder for the horses and lodging. However, the traders did not get to Europe themselves. They met with European traders (especially Italians) in the Middle East and exchanged goods. There is little evidence of Mongol traders actually resident in Europe. Ambassadors from Mongol-ruled countries sent to Europe tended not to be Mongols but were normally Europeans in Mongol service or Christians from subject populations. There were probably soldiers of Chinese origin in the Mongol armies as engineers.[16] In 1241 CE the Mongol army summered in Hungary and, unless Mongol soldiers were different from others, children of ethnically mixed parentage were born after they left. Extensive analysis of DNA samples from humans living in Eastern Europe[17] shows evidence of what is known as admixture with groups having ancestry from northeast Asia, including Mongolia. This indicates that the Mongols had a lasting impact upon Europe. After the summer respite, the Mongol army crossed the frozen Danube and there were further advances into Europe but these were reversed by the news of Ögedei's death. The history of Eastern Europe then enters a particularly complex phase when the playing of *chui wan* would have been a monstrous irrelevance.[18] By 1290 the Mongols lost interest in conquest and their direct influence in Europe was no more. The spread of *chui wan* during the process of brutal conquest is inherently unlikely and indeed it is also unlikely that any soldiers, a fairly lowly social group, played *chui wan* or knew anything about it. The presence of Mongol and Chinese soldiers in Hungary provides no clear channel for the transmission of the game from China to Europe.

There were Mongol 'slaves' in Europe[19] and their presence could have been a means of communication for the game of *chui wan*. However, the slaves were not ethnically Mongol but from one of the nations conquered by the Mongols. Possibly they were Tatars or Slavs who would have had no contact with the *chui wan*-playing Chinese elite. This, again, appears to be an unlikely channel of communication for anything Chinese. So far we have drawn a blank for obvious routes of communication of *chui wan* from China to Europe but there is a more promising avenue to explore.

European visitors

With the Mongols established as a major fighting force in the world there were a number of sophisticated European visitors to the court of the Khan. The reason for some visits was to enlist the Mongols in attempts to recover the city of Jerusalem from Moslem rule. We know about some of these visitors as they left written reports, but there may have been other visitors more concerned with trade and who left no record. As for cultural links between Europe and China, it is important to remember that they were envoys to the Mongol court, not to China proper.

Probably the first was John of Pian de Carprine,[20] who was despatched by Pope Innocent IV in 1245 CE. After much privation, he and his party reached the court of the Khan in Mongolia. The Khan declined the Pope's invitation to become a Christian and suggested that the Pope should swear allegiance to him. John returned emptyhanded in 1247. He made contact with only the Mongols and so the possibility that he saw *chui wan* being played is very small. As far as we know, Mongols never played *chui wan*; the nearest they got to game like that was playing polo on horseback, somewhat different from the genteel pastime of *chui wan*. Another visitor was André de Longjumea[21] who went to the Mongol court twice, in 1245 and in 1249 CE. He left no written record and we know about him only because of the writing of others. Ascelin of Lombardia[22] was another of the four missionaries Pope Innocent IV sent to the Mongol court in 1245. He was a stubborn man and was nearly killed because of his lack of respect for the Mongol rulers. After his meeting with the rulers by the Arax river, he returned to Europe with two Mongol companions and not much else.

A more significant visit was made by William of Rubruck in 1253 CE.[23] He reached the court of the Great Khan, Mŏngbe Khan, at Karakorum in 1254 CE. As the map indicates he did not even pass through China on his way to the court at Karakorum. On his return to King Louis IX of France he presented the king with a clear and precise account of his journey in which he describes the peculiarities of Mongolians as well as many geographical observations. There is no mention of stick-and-ball games. However, significantly for this study, he reports on the presence of a number of Europeans at the court including the nephew of an English bishop, a woman from Lorraine and a French silversmith.

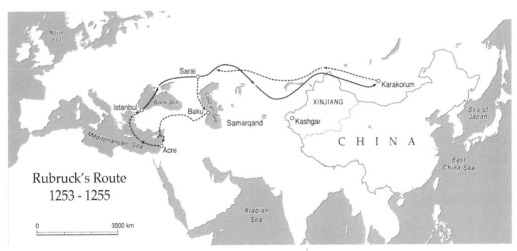

The journey of William of Rubruck in 1253 CE to the court of the Mongol Khan.

Marco Polo was the most famous European visitor to the Mongol court, although some scholars doubt that he ever reached China.

By far the most famous visitor to the Mongol Court was Marco Polo.[24] Marco's father and uncle first travelled to the Mongol court in the 1260s. They returned in 1275 with Marco and met Qubilai Khan at his summer palace at Shang Du. Marco was recruited as one of the many foreigners (not necessarily European) who administered the now Mongol–controlled country of China. He was there for 17 years but never learnt Chinese. When he returned to Europe he was imprisoned and while there dictated his memoirs to a fellow prisoner who, unfortunately for us, was a writer of romantic fiction. Marco describes some of the wonders of China but how much we should believe is difficult to say. Indeed there are some scholars[25] who think he did not get to China at all but learnt about it from others. This is a debate we need not enter for he does not mention stick-and-ball games. So, there is no indication from the writings of the official visitors that they saw *chui wan* being played.

Partly as a consequence of the Marco's visit, other merchants were soon to follow. The Florentine merchant Baldacci Pegolotti[26] compiled a guide to trade with China, based on the experience of other merchants who were well-versed in the exchange of goods with the Central Kingdom. A surgeon from Lombardy reached the city of Khambaliqin in 1303. In the Chinese port of Zaytun there was a small Genoese colony, mentioned by André de Pérouse.[27] Also resident in the city was Andalò da Savignone[28] who was sent to the West by the Khan in 1336 as part of the Mongol embassy to Pope Benedict XII. The Venetians were great traders and had a presence in China. In 1339 Giovanni Loredano returned to Venice after a stay in China and must have had much to relate but, unfortunately, we have no written record. Other traders are mentioned by Jackson.[29] There is also evidence that one set of Middle Eastern traders were resident on the Silk Road. A Hebrew prayer manual, of about 900 CE, was found in the great cache of manuscripts from the walled-up cave in the Buddhist grotto at Mogao, near the city of Dunhuang at the eastern end of the Silk Road.[30] Thus, there may have been a Jewish community there for the purpose of trade at that time. It seems not unreasonable to conclude from this brief survey that a substantial number of intelligent and observant Europeans visited China during the Yuan and early Ming dynasties. That they would have noted the leisure pastimes of the Chinese is certain; unfortunately few left any record of which we have current knowledge.

So, although the Chinese did not care to visit Europe, there were a fair number of Europeans, not envoys of the Pope but traders, who were eager to see and interact with China and the Chinese. Exactly how many we shall never know. The generally perceived isolation of China until recent time came about because of the chauvinism of the Chinese and has overlooked the inquisitive and entrepreneurial instincts of Europeans. The European visitors to China, we suggest, constitute the most likely channel for transmission of information about *chui wan* to Europe. The recent discovery of a Chinese skeleton in a Roman cemetery in London does not materially changes the situation. It is early, and probably that of a slave, not one of the cultivated middle classes who played *chui wan*.

Scottish links

For the last part of the journey, from continental Europe to the east coast of Scotland, the place seen by many as the 'birthplace' of modern golf, a possible route is much clearer as Scotland had a European trading partner: Flanders, now incorporated into the Netherlands. Although the large influx of Flemings (people from Flanders) into Scotland in the 11th century came largely through England, by the 13th century there was direct trade between Scotland and Flanders, including a large trade in wool. The earliest evidence of a 'special relationship' between the

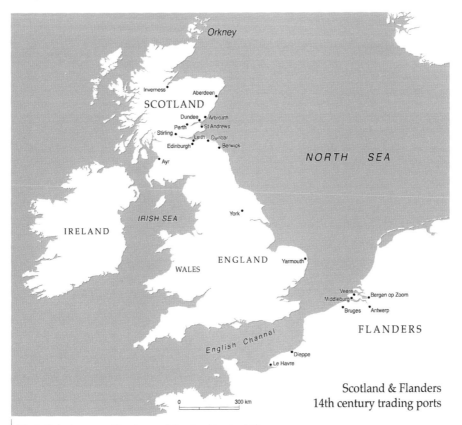

Trade links between Flanders and Scotland in the 14th century.

two countries is in a charter granted in 1182 to the monks of Melrose Abbey, great producers of wool, by Count Philip of Flanders by which the monks gained a right of passage through Flanders. The extent of the trade can be seen by the fact that, in the 13th century, King Edward 1 of England (the Hammer of the Scots) tried to undermine the success of the Scottish economy by the use of his influence in Flanders.[31] The frequent movement of merchants between the two countries means that any innovations in, or information about, stick-and-ball games in continental Europe could have reached the east coast of Scotland readily. The ports involved in the trade are shown in the map.[32]

From the discussion given above it is clear that the idea of China being completely isolated from the rest of the world during the European Middle Ages is not entirely accurate. The emergence of 'world history' as an important academic discipline has revealed the interconnectedness of different cultures throughout the world, not only in the European Middle Ages but even in the ancient world.[33] The Chinese may have cared little about the rest of humanity but many outside China were curious about this mysterious kingdom. There was much that warranted study: an ideographic language unlike anything in Europe, brilliant technological innovations and artistic achievements surpassing anything that Europe had accomplished by the Middle Ages. It also had a 'middle class', based on scholarship rather than inherited status, with the leisure and disposition to play a genteel game like *chui wan*. In principle, knowledge of *chui wan* could have reached the east coast of Scotland, the route becoming more and more certain as we move westwards. Whether there is evidence that this did occur we consider in Chapter 9.

References

1. Gui Yan, Zheng Tianju, Han Liebao, The study of chui wan, a golf-like game in the Song, Yuan and Ming dynasties of Ancient China, *J Sports History*, 2012, **39**, 283-297.

2. F Wood, *The Silk Road: Two Thousand Years in the Heart of Asia*, London, The Folio Society, 2002.

3. M A Stein, *Serindia*, London & Oxford, Clarendon Press, 1921, pp 669-677.

4. F Grenet, N. Sims-Williams & E dela Vaissière, The Sogdian ancient letter V, *Bull. Asia Institute*, 1998, 12, 91-104.

5. D Kuhn, *The Age of Confucian Rule*, Cambridge, Harvard University Press, 2011 p 190.

6. Surah al-Baqarah, 2: 219.

7. Ling Hongling, Verification of the fact that golf originated from chui wan. *Bull. Aust. Soc Sports Hist*, 1991, 12-22.

8. G Menzies, *1421 The Year China Discovered the World*, Bantam Press, London 2002.

9. R Finlay, How not to (re)write world history: Gavin Menzies and the Chinese discovery of America, *J World History*, 2004, 15, 229-242.

10. Zhao Rugao, *Zhu fan zhi (Records of Foreign People)*, China, 1225.

11. J Needham & Wang Ling, *Science and Civilisation in China. Vol. 5. Chemistry and Chemical Technology, Part 7, Military Technology,: the Gunpowder Epic*, Cambridge, CUP, 1987.

12. T F Carter, *The Invention of Printing in China and its Spread Westwards*, rev. L C Goodrich, New York, Ronald 1955.

13. Wu Linqi, Did Yuan Dynasty Mongols bring Golf Game into Europe? *Golfika* 8, 2011, 40-43.

14. F McLynn, *Genghis Khan*, London, The Bodley Head, 2015.

15. C P Attwood, *Encyclopedia of Mongolia and the Mongol Empire*, New York City, Facts on File, 2004, pp 90-93.

16. A Stewart, personal communication

17. G Hellenthal, G B J Busby, G Band, G F Wilson, C Capelli, D Falush & S Myers, A genetic atlas of human admixture history, *Science*, 2014, 343, 747-751.

18. C P Attwood, *Encyclopedia of Mongolia and the Mongol Empire*, New York City, Facts on File, 2004,

19. J L Abu-Lughod, *Before European Hegemony. The World System AD 1250-1350*, London, OUP, 1991.

20. C Dawson, *The Mongol Mission*, New York, Sheed & Ward, 1955.

21. I de Rachewiltz, *Papal Envoys to the Great Khan*, Stanford University Press, 1971, p 113.

22. J-P Roux, *Les Explorateurs au Moyen-Age*, Paris, Fayard, 1985, pp 97-98.

23. P Jackson (ed and trans), *The Mission of Friar William of Rubruck: His Journey to the Court of the Great Khan Möngke*, 1253-1255, ed D Morgan, London, Hakluyt Society. 1990.

24. Marco Polo, *The Description of the World*, trans and ed A C Moule and P Pelliot, 2 volumes, London, Routledge & Sons, 1938.

25. F Wood, *Did Marco Polo Go to China?* Colorado, Westview Press, 1998.

26. Francesco Balducci Pegolotti, *La practica della mercatura*, ed Allan Evans, Cambridge, Mediaeval Academy of America, 1936.

27. P Pelliot, *Chrétiens d'Asie Centrale et d'Extréme-Orient*, T'oung Pao, 1914.

28. G Meriana, *Andalò da Savignone. Un genovese alla corte del Gran Khan*, De Ferrari Editore, 2001.

29. P Jackson, *The Mongols and the West 1221-1410*, London, Longmans, 2005.

30. V Hansen, *Silk Road: a New History*, Oxford, OUP, 2012.

31. J Davidson & A Gray, *The Scottish Staple at Verre*, Longmans Green & Co, London, 1909.

32. W S Reid, *Skipper from Leith*, University of Pennsylvania Press, Philadelphia, 1962.

33. P Frankopan, *The Silk Roads: A New History of the World*, London, Bloomsbury, 2016.

CHUI WAN

Ming Dynasty Scroll
The Autumn Banquet

Chapter Nine:
The birthplace of golf: conclusions

Anthony Butler and David Hamilton

THERE are strong similarities between *chui wan* and modern golf but also many significant differences. Much has been made of the similarities; much less of the differences. If we are to trace the influence of *chui wan* on modern golf the two must be brought together and a balance sought. The two games have been compared in detail in Chapter 4 and that comparison is only summarised here. The aim of hitting a small solid object into a hole in the ground with the minimum number of strokes is clearly common to both games. The polite conduct of the players is another similarity but, in our opinion, only a limited significance should be attached to this, as good behaviour is common to almost all non-contact sports. There are uncanny similarities between some of the detailed rules of the two games in regard to anomalous situations, such as two balls landing very close to one another and of balls striking a player (Rule 11). Also significant is that, in both games, different clubs were, and are, used for different shots, an uncommon feature of stick-and-ball games, although seen in the French stick-and-ball game of *jeu de mail*.[1] In one form of this game, as in modern golf, two different clubs were used, one for the long, approach shot and one used in the more precise lofted strokes

There are a number of minor, but distinctive, features of *chui wan* that are also found in a few early European stick-and-ball games and, most conspicuously, in modern golf. The use of flags to locate the hole in *chui wan* is mentioned in Rule 8 and shown in the painting of the Emperor in Chapter 1. It is, of course, universal in modern golf. Although not used in modern golf, hitting the ball from a squatting position (mentioned in Rule 10) is shown in an illustration of a Flemish stick-and-ball game of c.1500.[2] In early modern golf a heap of sand was used as a tee for the first shot, a technique that is also used in *chui wan* although a broader 'base' of soil was used instead of sand (Rule 2). What can be deduced from these similarities will be discussed later.

The differences between the two games are as profound as the similarities. *Chui wan* does not use a pre-determined number of long holes for the game but this principle is an essential in golf, and there were a number of favourite Scottish coastal venues. The number of holes has not always been 18 (in 1764 St Andrews had only ten, of which eight were played twice) but it has always been a fixed and agreed number.[3] On the other hand, in *chui wan* just one hole could be used over and over again until one player has won the requisite number of playing tokens. Importantly, gambling is at the heart of *chui wan* but this is not the case in modern golf. Today's golf professionals may play for the sake of the prize money but for the thousands of amateur players throughout the world, it is a form of recreation and relaxation with only small stakes, if any. Critics may describe amateur golf as a 'good walk spoiled' but for most it is a 'good walk enhanced'. The scoring system in *chui wan* is akin to match play in golf but the award of playing tokens, depending on the number of strokes taken to hole the ball, has no parallel in modern golf. The complex rules governing the gambling aspect of *chui wan*, together with the penalties for irregular play, are detailed in Rules 13 and 14. In the light of these differences between the two games, *chui wan* does not appear to be an obvious precursor of modern golf. However, the similarities remain a tantalising puzzle.

Evolving Games

In considering the possibility of the knowledge of *chui wan* passing from China to Europe, there is a factor not present in the history of, for example, gunpowder and printing, two inventions that did make the journey from China to the West. In contrast to the very considerable technological innovation required for both printing and gunpowder, the basic technology of hitting a small object towards a target, be it a hole (as in golf), at a hoop (as in croquet) or a goal (as in hockey) is so simple that it can hardly be described as an invention. It is discovered by children playing together in every generation. We will call this basic play the 'simple game'. Some variant of the simple game is probably played in every country in the world. That the Greeks played a simple stick-and-ball game is clear and early travellers in the Dutch East Indies saw natives playing a ball game with sticks, as did explorers in Chile.[4] The general view is that all human societies throughout the world turned, in times of leisure, to hit balls with sticks. It was the sophistication of the simple game that has led to the range of elaborate stick-and-ball games we now know. The path the sophistication took depends upon a number of factors, including the nature of the terrain and the character of the people.

The Mongols were skilled horsemen and lived in vast open grasslands. Polo is a likely end product of the process of sophistication of the simple game. Where horsemanship was not the abiding passion of the people, as in Iran, but where there was space, field hockey was a more likely development. In the Netherlands, a rather crowded country and where a rare open space suitable for sport was a frozen canal, a street game, known as *colf*, was sometimes played on ice and the ball was pushed rather than struck, as in modern ice hockey.

In *chui wan, pu* clubs were used for air shots and *cuan* clubs for ground shots (Rule 10). Unfortunately, at the moment, we have no information on how the design of these clubs differed, and terms like eagle-beak are not very helpful, but it is likely that the clubs bore some resemblance to the woods of modern golf. We are not sure what to make of *shao* clubs for one-arm shots (Rule 11).

How does this idea work when we consider sophistication of the 'simple game' in China? There was much intensive agriculture in China as early as the Tang dynasty and so free space where people lived was not abundant and the special features of *chui wan* (frequently only one hole) would be appropriate. If it were played in the palace grounds, as suggested by the two paintings mentioned in Chapter 1, then a restriction in the number of holes becomes a necessity. The scoring system used in *chui wan* turns the simple game into a gambling game, a passion right at the heart of the Chinese character. A short passage from the *The Travels of Marco Polo* describing his time in China captures that passion. He writes:

> *The present grand khan has prohibited all species of gambling and other modes of cheating, to which the people of this country [China] are addicted more than any others on earth; and as an argument for deterring them from the practice, he says (in his edict) 'I subdued you by the power of my sword, and consequently whatever you possess belongs of right to me: if you gamble therefore you are sporting with my property.'* [6]

How successful this edict was is not known but it may have contributed to the decline in playing *chui wan* as the game died out some time in the Ming dynasty (1368-1644). Nevertheless, the propensity of the Chinese for gambling is entirely consistent with the development of the scoring system (the collection of playing tokens) used in *chui wan*. It might be suggested that it makes *chui wan* as close to poker as to other stick-and-ball games. There is also the calculated risk taken in selecting the location (the back, middle or front of the playing area) for the first shot of each hole. There is nothing comparable to that in modern golf.

As was described in Chapter 6, the simple game was played in Scotland in the churchyard after the Sunday service (named as 'the short game'). Aristocrats did not participate in this game but did develop a more sophisticated or 'long game'. This involved an initial long drive towards the hole, followed by a short shots to get the ball into the hole. The initial drive was possible because, in many coastal towns in sparsely populated medieval Scotland, there was a strip of land between the town and the coast, known as the links. The links were used for a variety of purposes from horse fairs to drying and washing and remained in good condition in winter. This gave the Scottish game its distinctive character, links golf, a game that has since developed into the highly sophisticated game of modern golf with devotees in almost every country in the world. Although both *chui wan* and Scottish long golf may have had a common origin in the simple game, they apparently developed independently according to the terrain of the country and the tastes of the populace. But was the development completely independent? This is a matter to which we shall return.

The Gunpowder Saga

An extremely important invention that did make the journey from China to Europe, around the time that *chui wan* was being played, is gunpowder. It consists, as every mischievous schoolboy used to know, of a mixture of sulphur, carbon and saltpetre (potassium nitrate). The explosive nature of such a mixture was probably discovered accidently by Chinese alchemists in the eighth century CE as they experimented with countless mixtures of naturally occurring substances in the search for new medicinal drugs. The Chinese for gunpowder is *huo yao*, meaning 'fire medicine'. However, its deflagrating and explosive properties quickly led to it being used in fireworks, military flame throwers, canons and in civil engineering. From printed sources in China in the period 1044 to 1350 CE a wide range of recipes for gunpowder is reported, with very different proportions of the three components. However, later recipes give only the optimum mixture for maximum explosive capability. Gunpowder became known in Europe in the thirteenth century and the formula given was always that of the optimum mixture. Nowhere in Europe is there evidence of experimentation in the proportions of the components. One of the early users of gunpowder in Europe was Francis Bacon and he had been a fellow student in Paris with William of Rubruck, a visitor to China (Chapter 8) and this could have a route for the transmission of gunpowder to Europe.[7]

So, it is most probable that gunpowder was not invented independently in both Europe and China; it was a Chinese invention that trave, led to Europe. Had *chui wan* been introduced into Europe in the same way, this recogniable, viable, mature and entertaining stick-and-ball game would have appeared prominently in the records; it did not.

Envoi

The arguments used above suggest that *chui wan* was not introduced into Europe in its entirety. However, any one of the many European visitors to China, discussed in Chapter 8, might have seen *chui wan* being played, noted any features that were special or innovative and brought that information back to Europe. It could then have been passed on to the players of any of the stick-and-ball games being played at that time and utilised in the sophistication of that game. This is particularly significant in Scotland for the metamorphosis of the short game, played by artisans, into the long game played by nobility using the expanses of favourable turf on the links. If these features were learnt from the playing of *chui wan*, that game has a part in the development of modern golf. So although it would be wrong to see China as the birthplace of golf, it is possible that some features essential to modern golf are of Chinese origin, notably the variety of clubs in use, their hybrid wooden construction and some of the rules. If this is suggestion is correct, China has every right to claim some credit for enhancing the development of the short game into what has become modern golf. Now, of course, golf is international and, for most players, its origins are of only passing interest but let us cherish the memories of the Chinese who, long ago, developed techniques that may have made a significant contribution to the development of the game of golf as we now know it. So little is known about the game from Chinese sources, that any conclusion we reach concerning the relationship between *chui wan* and modern golf must be tentative.

References

1. *New Rules for the Game of Mail*, Paris 1717.

2. *The Golf Book* ca 1500, BL Add.MS 24098.

3. David Hamilton, *Golf - Scotland's Game*, Partick Press, Kilmacolm 1998, p. 62.

4. F Frezier, *A Voyage to the South-Seas*, London 1717.

5. Olive M Geddes, *A Swing Through Time: Golf in Scotland 1457-1744*, NMS, Edinburgh 2007.

6. *The Travels of Marco Polo*, Book 2, Chapter XXVI.

7. Joseph Needham and Ho Pingyu, *Science and Civilisation in China*, Cambridge University Press, Cambridge, 1986.

Mural from the Shuishan
Temple in Shanxi Province

Chapter Ten:
Translation of *Wan Jing*

Chuan Gao and Wuzong Zhou

丸经上卷	*Wan Jing* [1] Vol 1
承式章第一	**Rule 1. Inheriting traditional rules**
捶丸之制，全式为上，破式次之，违式出之。（捶丸之式，先习家风，后学体面。折旋中矩，周旋中规，失利不嗔，得隽不逞。若喜怒见面，利口伤人，君子不与也。）	**There are regulations for *chui wan*.[2] It is best if players fully follow the regulations. It is not good if players break some of the regulations. Anyone violates the regulations should be expelled from the game.** (The regulations for playing are that a player must first learn and practise the traditional morality of play and then learn the etiquette of the game. Players must follow the rules and moral norms and must be polite when playing back and forth and meeting other players on the playing area. Players must not get angry when they lose and must not show off when they win. Anyone showing either pleasure or anger on his face, or making sharp statements, is not a genial companion of gentlemen.)
让采索窝，（让人先抛球儿，得采者便索窝。）	**Throw the balls to see who has the first stroke.** (Let others throw the ball first out of politeness. The person who hits the target has first stroke of the game.)
忘撺成算。（手中无撺者，算输一筹，无鹰嘴同。）	**Forgetting to bring a *cuan* club[3] is an offence.** (If a player has no *cuan* club to use, he loses one token. No *eagle-beak* club[4] leads to the same consequence, i.e. to lose one token.)
因动为击，（球儿基上安定，或被风吹动，当称风落。如不称风落，或自那动者，亦算打了。）	**If the ball moves it counts as a stroke.** (A ball is placed on a base. If the ball moves away from the base because of wind, it is known as *blown off (feng luo)*. If it is not the case of *blown off* or the ball is moved by the player, both count as a stroke.)
对权不易。（对定球棒，不可换易。或再换及抹去圮子者，亦算输一筹。）	**After selecting a club to play with, the player cannot change it.** (It is not permitted to change clubs just before hitting the ball. If a player does change club or removes an obstacle in front of the ball, he loses one token.)
乖令背式，罚不可恕。（他人得胜，索着法度不依随者，算输一筹。球儿打在窝中，用棒拨出者，输一筹。）	**Disobeying the regulations and ignoring the traditional style of play should be punished without forgiveness.** (As an example, a player loses a playing token if he seeks excuse to not accept that other player has won according to the regulations. If he removes an opponent's ball from the hole with a club, he will lose one token.)
趋时争利，赏不为加。（自己球儿在不得墒处，却那在便利之墒，不赏而有罚。）	**If a player seize the chance to get an advantage, he will not be rewarded.** (If a player moves his ball from a less advantageous place to a more advantageous place, it should still be punished rather than rewarded.)
胜负靡常，色斯举矣。（赢即矜能逞语，输即发怒便走，或至骂仆嗔朋，抛球掷棒。此非闲雅君子，真小人耳。俚语云：废球棒，磨靴底；眼睛饱，肚里饥；桦皮脸，拖狗	**The result of game is not foreseeable. The players should not gloat or show anger.** (If the winners boast, the losers leave the course in a fit of rage or take it out on servants or blame friends, or throw balls and clubs, then they are not elegant and gentle people. In fact, they are villains. A slang says: throwing away or damaging clubs in anger and stumping or kicking the ground in anger, satisfying the eye but leaving the mind unfulfilled, being cheeky and shameless, boasting

皮；输便怒，赢便喜；吃别 人，不回礼。此之谓也。）	when they win and angering when they lose, enjoying being invited to dinner and never hosting dinner in return. All these behaviours mark villains.)

[1] '*Wan*' means ball or ball game. '*Jing*' means book. Therefore the title of this booklet can be understood as: The Book of the Ball Game.
[2] '*chui*' means strike. Therefore, '*chui wan*' means to play ball.
[3] '*cuan*' originally means 'throw' and here it is one type of clubs specially designed for the game.
[4] '*eagle-beak*' is another type of club. It is also called '*shao*' club.

崇古章第二	Rule 2. Respecting ancient style
灵台潜虚，较若画一；会 其至当，精艺无二。（人心 随时更异，谓如窝脚、会儿本 自一家，今分两处。窝脚只使 撺棒，能走、能飞、能收窝， 法度更多，人不易学。会儿只 打扑棒，能飞不能走，又不能 收窝，法度更少，人甚易学。 此今人之说，上古未闻。然则 今人多有自家不晓诸般法度， 只说别人是窝脚。殊不知艺到 精处，同一理而已，岂有差 别？）	'*Ling Tai*' [1] and '*Qian Xu*' [2] might be equally excellent. When skills are developed to a superb level, their differences become insignificant. (People tend to change their minds as time passes. For example, the *Wo-jiao* and the *Hui-er* [3] players were originally in one organisation, but have now split into two. In the *Wo-jiao* group, players only use *cuan* clubs for all shots, chip shots, long shots, and for putting. This group has more complicated rules than the others and the rules are difficult to learn. In contrast, the *Hui-er* players use *pu* clubs [4] only, which can make long shots, but not chip shots and putting. Also the *Hui-er* group has fewer rules, making it easier for people to learn. This difference is only commonly mentioned by people today, but was never heard in former time. Nowadays people do not realise that there are various sets of regulations and simply complain that others are *Wo-jiao*. They do not realise that when the players' skills approach a very high level, the standard of evaluation becomes the same. Why care about their differences?)
先登者,生之徒,后撞者, 死之计。（先有人二棒打在窝 边，后来人二棒误撞前球，不 问有画无画，先活后死，故意 打去撞人者，算输一筹。）	The first ball landing has priority to stay. The ball hitting the first will be removed. (If the first player lands the ball near the hole with the second stroke and then the ball is hit by the second stroke of the second player, no matter whether this action is planned or not, the ball of the first player should be returned to where it was. At the same time, as a penalty, the ball of the second player should be removed. If the second player hit the first player's ball on purpose, he loses one token.)
逾堄越纵，从累其主。（球 儿著身者，若在堄上行者死了 球儿；但是伴当在堄上行走 者，死了本官球儿。不在堄上 著人，无伤。）	Retinues of players walking through the playing field may implicate the players. (If a player's ball strikes an opponent's supporter who is on the playing area, the opponent loses. If the ball strikes one of the player's own supporters, the player loses. If a ball strikes someone outside the playing area, there is no penalty.)
放土安基。随堄起垒。（倒 棒、正棒，基中安下垫棒，棒 上不放土者，自死一筹。土尖 垒起，样子有添无减，捶者若 将棒于顶上按实，即算输一 筹。球上球、翻杖、撅儿、皮 塔儿、砖角等，不放干土索窝	It is permitted to use earth to raise the ground for the starting base according to the lay of the playing field. (For *dao-bang* and *zheng-bang*, [5] one may place sticks on the base. If no soil is put on the sticks, the player loses without playing. Using soil to make a mound, the height seems increased. Players may not use a club to compact the mound. Otherwise, the penalty is to lose one token. There are various advanced techniques of playing such as *ball-on-ball*, *turning-stick*, *poking*, *pi-ta-er*, *brick-corner*, etc. [6] If not using dry soil on the hole,

者，自死一筹。诸杂巧捶，皮面打著球儿者，皆是活球。若是本分著球者，谓之上棒，死球也。）	the player loses one token without playing. In many advanced strokes, if the ball is hit by the leather head of the club, it is counted as a valid stroke and the game can continue. If, on the other hand, it is hit by the wooden part of the club, called *up-the-stick*, it is not a valid stroke.)
矜能丧善， （有等人说，捶丸时只是高强打处便赢，未尝有输。及到场上，口中说得精细，手拙不能应口，一筹不展，全场输了。俚语云："高者不说，说者不高。"是也。）	**Conceit may lose players' good behaviour.** (Some players say that high skills are the only thing they need to win *chui wan*. They would never lose. However, on the playing field, what they say is much better than what they can do. They cannot demonstrate any excellent skills and they often lose the whole game. A slang says: The talented remain silent, while the unskilled boast. It is truly correct for these people.)
方欺苟瞒。 （有等人，场上引著十余伴当，将一般颜色球儿打在死处，却放一个在好处，做活球；又去打行处带踏圳子，在死处，踢在活处。俟人眼不见，把他人球儿踢在死处，小厮每踏在土里，然后拿死球。如此者，真可耻也。）	**Players will not get away with cheating for very long.** (Some players lead more than ten retinues on the playing field. When their balls land in a 'dead' place, they put a ball with the same colour in a good place to replace the 'dead' one. They may also go to the 'dead' place, trampling a bump and kicking the ball to a good place. When nobody notices, they kick the opponent's ball to a 'dead' place and even stamp the ball down to the ground, and then collect it as a 'dead' ball. Players having such behaviours are really shameful.)
挂窝住傍，致疑成隙。 （凡棒柄窝上横过抹著球儿，算挂窝，抹不着，算上球儿。打在住处傍边上，画记，定教人远看，不要到根前，本不那动，教人猜疑，遂成嫌隙。）	**It is easy to arouse suspicion if the ball is found to be on the lip of the hole or very near it.** (When a ball lands on the lip of the hole, the player strikes the ball into the hole with the club crossing the hole. This is called *hanging-at-hole*. If the ball is not touched, it is called *over-ball*. When a ball lands near the hole, the player needs to make a mark. If the player only allows people to have a view from a long distance instead of a close look, even he does not move the ball, other people will be suspicious.)
因人上画。 （球儿被人踢动，只教本人上画。若是自家上画，死了球儿。）	**Let other people to mark the original position of the ball in case it is kicked by him.** (If your ball is kicked by someone that person should mark the original position of the ball. If you make the mark by yourself it counts as a 'dead' ball.)
正赛诡随。 （今人口巧手拙，但打得诡随，不得正赛之规度，怎争胜负？心懵懂，性刚燥，强辩不伏，自害惶恐。俚语云：有智赢，无智输。只此是也。）	**Sly behaviour during a formal game.** (There are people nowadays who are good at talking about play but not skilful at all in practice. They resort to tricks. As they have no knowledge of the regulations how can they join the competition? These people are ignorant, stubborn and hot-tempered, always arguing and are defensive and jittery. There is a slang saying: Being ready to accept success, but not able to accept failure. This is a description of such people.)
览而记之，神斯会矣。 （熟看此书，自然捶击诸法，众皆敬服，岂不快哉！）	**Read and understand this book and you will be able to play well.** (On reading this book repeatedly you will gain the skill of playing and receive the respect from others. Is that not an enjoyable thing?)

[1] 'Ling Tai ' is a poem in 'The Book of Songs' before Qin Dynasty, 221-206 BCE.
[2] 'Qian Xu' is a book by Sima Guang, a high-ranking scholar-official and historian in Song Dynasty, 960-1279 CE.
[3] 'Wo-jiao' and 'Hui-er' are the names of two *chui wan* societies at that time.

[4] '*pu*' is one type of club.
[5] '*dao-bang*' and '*zheng-bang*' are two principal manners of holding club before striking. '*bang*' means club. '*dao*' means tilting or lying down. '*zheng*' means standing.
[6] '*ball-on-ball*', '*turning-stick*', '*poking*', '*pi-ta-er*', '*brick-corner*', are different techniques of putting. The details of each movement are not known.

审时章第三	**Rule 3. Choosing times and seasons for play**
作有时，（天朗气清，惠风和畅，饫饱之余，心无所碍，取择良友三三五五，于园林清胜之处，依法捶击。风雨阴晦、大寒大暑，不与也。）	**Suitable time for playing *chui wan*.** (A sunny day with clean air. Gentle wind makes people feel comfortable. After a good meal, without any worries in mind, one may invite a few good friends to a quiet and beautiful place to play *chui wan* according to the regulations. When it is raining, windy, dark, obscure, very hot or very cold, it is not suitable for the game.)
乐有节。（议定会数，或五或七，会满为止。惟在和血脉，养性情、涤烦襟、消饮食而已，勿为荒逸。）	**Entertainments should be moderate.** (Before starting the game, its number of sets should be decided, such as either five or seven. When the sets are completed, the game should be terminated. The purposes of playing *chui wan* are improving bodily circulation, attaining mental and emotional tranquillity, eliminating worry and aiding digestion. Do not overdo it.)
有时则事不废，（知时为嬉，则不误事。）	**By choosing a right time for playing, normal work will not be neglected.** (Knowing when you can play will not affect other parts of your life.)
有节则志不妨。（既不荒逸，志不邪矣。）	**By controlling and moderating play, aspirations of the players will not be thwarted.** (If playing time are carefully controlled, personal ambition will not be adversely affected.)
无时无节，则事废而志妨；有时有节，则身安而志逸。（不得其时，则荒废政事、伤气动志；得其时，则心平气和、志自乐矣。）	**If time and length of play are not carefully considered it will displace work and the career ambitions of the players will not be achieved. If the time and length of play are well controlled, the players become physically fit and their minds relaxed.** (If time of play is not carefully selected, the players will neglect official business, lose their tempers and thwart their ambitions. On the other hand, if the time of play is carefully selected, the players will be calm, cheerful and in high spirits.)

因地章第四	**Rule 4. The playing area**
地形有平者、有凸者、有凹者、有峻者、有仰者、有阻者、有妨者、有迎者、有里者、有外者。（诸形绝无曰平，龟背曰凸，中低曰凹，势颇曰峻，之上曰仰，前隔曰阻，后碍曰妨，可反曰迎，左高曰里，右高曰外。）	**The playing area may have varied terrain: *flat, raised, concave, steep down, slope up, blocked in front, hindered behind, rebound, inward or outward*.** (Ground with no special features is called *flat*. If it protrudes upwards, like the back of a turtle, it is called *raised*. A depression is described as *concave*. If the ground falls sharply it is called *steep down*. A gentle upwards incline is called *slope up*. An obstruction in front of the ball is called *blocked in front*. If an obstruction is behind the ball, it is called *hindered behind*. If the ground causes the ball to run backwards it is a *rebound*. An incline from one side

	to another, with the left side higher is called *inward* but if the right side is higher it is called *outward*.)
平者勿失，（地形平，则众皆可及。我既及家，众若失家，则败。）	**When ground is flat, do not make mistakes.** (If the ground is flat everyone can hole the ball. But if I am the first to achieve this, the others are losers.)
凸者有取，（形如龟背，难从中形，必观左右形势而取用。）	**When the ground is raised, the way to play should be carefully chosen.** (When the ground is raised like the back of a turtle, it is difficult to go through the middle. Instead, the left and right side topography must be viewed and one of the pathways should be selected.)
凹者有行，（两高中低，可从中行，到家不难。）	**If the ground is depressed, you can play straight through.** (If the ground is higher on both sides than in the middle it is not difficult to pass the ball through the middle.)
峻者欲缓，（球住峻坡，窝在坡下，不可力击，轻缓击之。）	**If there is a steep downwards your stroke should be gentle.** (If the ball lands at the top of a slope and the hole is at the bottom, do not hit the ball too strongly. Instead, hit it gently.)
仰者欲及，（窝在上，球在下，不到则不能上，必使到窝边落也。）	**Trying to hole the ball when the approach to the hole is an upward slope.** (If the hole is on an upward slope and the ball is at the bottom, it is not near enough to hole. Therefore, effort should be made to land the ball close to the hole.)
阻者欲越，（窝与球相隔，必高超可至。）	**Go over the block when it is in front of the ball.** (If there is block between the ball and the hole, hit the ball high, so that it goes over the block towards the hole.)
妨者用巧，（后既有碍，难于运棒。当取地形，对棒端正，）	**When there is a hindrance behind, use the club skilfully.** (A hindrance behind the ball makes it difficult to swing the club. Investigate the terrain and use the club carefully by getting the club in the best position.)
迎者勿及，（窝后有墙壁或木石者，不可定至窝边落，恐迎回无功，）	**When there is an item behind the hole that might cause the ball to rebound, do not allow the ball to touch it.** (When there is a wall or a fence behind the hole do not land the ball around the hole without considering this circumstance, as it may rebound and waste your effort.)
里者里之，（吾左高，窝在右，当反里之，就其势，）	**In an 'inward' situation, use the slope accordingly.** (When the left hand side is higher and the hole is at the right, hit the ball in the direction of the slope and let it roll down into the hole.)
外者外之。（吾右高，窝在左，当反外之，就其势。）	**In an 'outward' situation, use the slope accordingly.** (If the right hand side is higher and the hole is at the left, hit the ball in the direction of the slope on right and let it roll down into the hole.)
立飞者囊，（撲棒单手，盛于革囊也，）	**Long clubs for distance shots are stored in a bag.** (*Pu* clubs, single-hand, are stored in a leather bag.) [1]

行蹲者籠。（撣棒、杓棒盛于提籃也。）	**Short clubs used when crouching are stored in a basket.** (*Cuan* clubs and *shao* clubs are kept in a basket). [2]
所称既备，无不胜矣。（凡称心之棒既全有，已如此者，无有不胜之道也。）	**Having prepared all the relevant equipment mentioned above, you cannot lose.** (There is no reason why anyone, who has all the appropriate clubs in place, should not win.)

[1] '*Pu* club' is a type of long club. However, it is not known whether 'single-hand' means the '*pu* clubs' are used by one hand or it is a name of another type of club.
[2] '*Cuan*' and '*shao*' are two types of short clubs.

择利章第五	**Rule 5. Playing according to circumstances**
土有坚者、有垒者、有燥者、有湿者。（地之形也。）	**The playing ground may be hard or fluffy, dry or wet.** (These are the characteristics of the playing ground.)
坚者损之，（土硬球难止，力大则远，故减力而击之。）	**When the ground is hard, players should reduce the power of a stroke.** (If the ground is hard, the ball rolls farther and powerful strokes will make the ball go too far. Therefore, less strength should be applied.)
垒者益之，（土松球难行，故加力击之。）	**When the ground is loose, the power of a stroke should be increased.** (On soft ground a ball rolls with greater difficultly and a more powerful stroke should be used.)
燥者，湿者，随形处之。（观土燥湿，随地宜而击。）	**Play according to the state of the ground, wet or dry.** (Assess the degree of wetness or dryness of the ground and play accordingly. Players benefit by making a stroke appropriate to the ground conditions.)
因地之利，制胜之道也。（得地利之宜，亦取胜之一端也。）	**Taking advantages of the ground is important in winning the game.** (Players benefit by making a stroke appropriate to the ground conditions. This is one of the critical factors of winning.)

定基章第六	**Rule 6. Establishing the base** [1]
基，纵不盈尺，横亦不盈尺。(纵，长也；横，阔也，皆不满一尺也。)	**The base area should be no more than one *che* [2] in both vertical and horizontal directions.** (The vertical direction means the length of the base area and the horizontal direction means the width of the base area. Both are less than one *che*.)
择地而处之，（拣好地画基。）	**First select the site and then establish the base area.** (Select a good place and draw lines to indicate the base area.)
直向而画之，（直对窝也。）	**Draw the base along the vertical direction.** (The vertical direction points to the hole.)

[81]

瓦砾则除之。（若有瓦砾草木等物，除毕然后画基。）	**Rubbles should be removed.** (Any rubble, grass or wood should be removed before drawing the base area.)
权弯者利陷，（船样棒不利剑脊基，偏利碟样基。）	**Clubs with a curved head [3] are suitable for a sunken base area.** (Clubs with upturned boat shaped heads are not suitable for a raised base shaped like face of a sword. But it is specially suitable for a base shaped like a plate, the middle is lower than the edges.)
权直者利凸。（棒直不利碟样基，偏利剑脊基。）	**Clubs with a straight head are suitable for a raised base.** (Straight clubs are not suitable for a plate-like base. But it is specially suitable for a sword-face shaped base.)
作基不左立，（假如向南击球，画基者不得居西，可居东。）	**The base should not be set up on the left hand side of a player.** (If a player intends to hit the ball to the south, he should stand on the east side of the base, not on the west.)
丸不处基外。（球安在基外者败。）	**A ball must never be placed outside the base area.** (Who doing so loses the game.)
权不击基，（画毕及未画，不可基内试棒。）	**Clubs should not be swung within the base area.** (No matter whether the lines of the base area have been completely drawn or not, there should be no hitting of practice balls within the base area once it has been selected.)
足不踏基，手不拭基，无易基。（恐利他也。）	**Players must not step on the base area or wipe it by hand. It must not be changed to another place.** (Someone might benefit from these actions.)
无毁基。（禁恶徒也。）	**Once the base area has been set up, there it must remain.** (This prevents villains destroying other people's bases.)
后碍家傍不处基。（后碍损棒，难运窝傍，复来难为。）	**Do not set a base facing in a direction near the hole where there is a hindrance behind.** (A hindrance behind the base may damage the club and it is difficult to get the ball towards the hole. As it is a difficult shot, even repeating cannot help much.)
不践家傍，恐有作也。（窝边周围五尺内不许人行，恐凶恶之徒埇土阻球，作坑陷球。窝边行者，同班皆输。）	**Do not walk to the land near the hole, as people may cheat with it.** (It is not permitted to walk within five *che* of a hole. This prevents bad people from cheating by piling up earth in the path of the ball or digging holes to trap opponents' balls. Walking around the hole results in a loss for the whole team.)
故动复择基，两反不许作，（倘有同班，一球在左、一球在右，所住难为，彼同类者，故为不得已而动之，动已，复拣好基，如此者，将动球人来往两遭，不许击球。）	**Moving balls on purpose and relocating the base area should be punished by missing two turns of play.** (When balls from two players of the same team land next to each other, one on the left and another on the right, it is difficult to continue play. Since the other player is in the same team and one of the balls must be removed, a player may intentionally move his own ball to a better base. When he does this, the player should be punished by missing two turns of stroke.)

此御奸之术也。(禁虚诈奸恶之法也。)	**All these rules are established to prevent fraudulent behaviour.** (These regulations prevent bad behaviour such as falsifying, offending and other bad actions.)

[1] '*Ji*', means base. It is a special prepared place for the first stroke.
[2] '*Che*' is a unit of length in Chinese, which is about 1/3 of a meter and slightly longer than foot.
[3] Direct translation from Chinese characters gives 'bent club' (this sentence) and 'straight club' (next sentence). However, these do not make sense.

取友章第七	**Rule 7. Selecting fellow players**
恭必泰，(恭敬者必安祥。)	**Being respectful must lead to being serene.** (Respectful people must be peaceful and serene.)
浮必乱。(轻浮者必争乱。)	**Being superficial must lead to being disorganised.** (Superficial and impetuous people are always disorganised and will cause arguments.)
泰者，善之徒，(君子也。)	**Peaceful people are kind people.** (They are people of noble characters.)
乱者，恶之徒。(小人也。)	**Disorganised people are vicious and ignoble people.** (They are the villains.)
君子小人，其争也不同，其朋也有异。(君子小人，其志不同，在人识察之也。)	**Gentlemen and villain, their objectives are different, and their friends are also different.** (Gentlemen people and villain, their ambitions are different. Therefore, it is important to carefully observe their behaviours during the games.)
君子之争，艺高而服众，(技艺高，人自服。)	**Competitions between gentlemen are always about their skills of play and they win respect by their excellent skills.** (Players with a high level technical skills are automatically admired by other players.)
小人之争，奇诈而谋利。(技艺低，以诈取利。)	**In competition between villains, they use odd tricks in order to gain advantage.** (Players with poor technical skills employ tricks to gain an advantage.)
是故会朋，必以君子而远小人也。(必进君子，退小人。)	**Therefore, you should make friends with the gentlemen and stay far away from the villains.** (Keep close to worthy players but repulse the villains.)
昔楚庄王为匏居之台，宴者、相者、赞者、而皆贤者，伍举称之。(称其能会贤人也。)	**In old time, *Chu Zhuang Wang* [1] constructed a large stage, *Pao Ju Tai*, for rituals. Since all the people in a feast, including the invited guests, officials and speakers on ceremony, were all able and virtuous people. *Wu Ju* [2] praised.** (What *Wu Ju* praised was that The King was able to make friends with worthy people.)

灵王为章华之台，宴者、相者、赞者，皆非贤者，伍举谏之。（谏其不得贤人，而所近者小人也。）	*Ling Wang*, [3] built *Zhang Hua Tai* for entertainment. All the people in a feast, including the invited guests, officials and speakers, were not able and virtuous people. *Wu Ju* **admonished.** (What *Wu Ju* admonished was that the King was unable to work with worthy people, and people surrounding him were all unworthy people.)
捶丸会朋，不可不慎也。（捶丸虽为聚娱，险佞之人，不可与同乐也。君子慎之。）	**One has to be cautious when one meets friends in playing** *chui wan*. (Although *chui wan* is a game for people to assemble for enjoying themselves, do not play with treacherous people. All gentlemen must be cautious in choosing fellow players.)

[1] 'Chu Zhuang Wang' The King of the State of *Chu* in *Chun Qiu* period (618－591 BCE),
[2] 'Wu Ju' was an important civil official in the State of *Chu*.
[3] 'Ling Wang' was another King of the State of *Chu* (~529 BCE).

正仪章第八	Rule 8. Playing according to etiquette
剮场建旗，（球场上剮成了窝，立彩色旗儿。）	**Dig hole(s) in the playing field and insert flag(s).** (Set up coloured flags in the holes to make the field of play.) [1]
合众同乐。（合聚捶丸之人，相与同乐。）	**The party should play as a group and share the entertainment derived.** (People come together to play *chui wan* and share their happiness.)
恪慎其仪，各事其事。（各人谨守进退，各去关牌领筹。）	**Everyone must play strictly by the rules and do what they should do.** (All must know their position and go to the ticket-office to collect playing tokens.)
奔竞躁逸，（争取筹棒，夸口逞手。）	**Rushing forward and running about impatiently,** (Snatching tokens and clubs, boasting and showing off.)
号呶喧哗，（在场闹噪叫嚣。）	**shouting and clamouring,** (shouting and clamouring when playing *chui wan*.)
比于败群，不可与也。（如此之人，不循规矩，是如败群搅众，即逐去之。）	**make these people unworthy players and they should not be approached.** (These people, who do not abide by the regulations and disturb others, should be asked to leave the field of play immediately.)
有斐君子，其仪不忒，（如有文质君子，依守规式，自有容仪，不至差失。）	**Players with literary talent and honesty are acceptable, both in appearance and manners.** (For example, worthy people, who are gentle and comply with all regulations, accordingly have already showed their good appearances and etiquette without any mistakes.)
安如闲如，（容止安详。）	**People who appear peaceful and calm must behave accordingly, in a relaxed, cheerful and elegant manner.** (It indicates that their appearances and behaviours are serene and charming.)

夭如申如，周旋闲雅。（转旋动作，夭夭申申如也。）	**They are relaxed, cheerful and elegant.** (They are elegant when they turn their body to strike the ball.)
不劳神于极，以畅四肢。（不太任力，至于疲乏，但要得四体血脉和畅而已。）	**Do not get too tired and allow all four limbs to relax.** (Do not play extensively, becoming exhausted. The purpose of playing *chui wan* is to improve circulation in the limbs.)
非手之舞之，足之蹈之耶？（所以怡悦性情，使自娱乐耶。）	**Don't you think that playing *chui wan* has the same consequences as dancing which is also based on the movement of legs and arms?** (Playing makes people happy and allows them to entertain themselves.)

[1] 'Wo' means home. Here it means hole. In the text, it says to set up coloured flags. However, it is not mentioned set up flags in the holes or around the field. We believe they are more likely in the holes.

置序章第九	**Rule 9. Deciding the order of play**
初击者择基而安，（头棒安基。）	**The player who is going to make the first stroke chooses a place to set a base.** (Set up a base for the first stroke.)
其次随处而作。（二棒随球住处便击，不许安基，安则败。）	**The second stroke takes place wherever the ball lands from the first stroke.** (The second stroke starts at the position where the ball lands and you are not allowed to set up another base for the second stroke. Anyone doing this loses the game.)
其次择基谓之强，（二棒安基者，强梁之徒也。）	**Anyone making a base for the second stroke is presumptuous.** (Anyone insisting on setting up a base for the second stroke is a bully.)
初击不容谓之阻。（头棒不许人安基者，是阻人能也。）	**Anyone not allowing others to set up their bases for the first stroke is guilty of obstruction.** (This is because not allowing free choice stops other players from achieving their best.)
强者，君子恶之，小人作之。（强阻之辈，君子不悦，小人为能。）	**People who do this are disliked by worthy players, but likely followed by unworthy people.** (Honest players are unhappy with those who obstruct, but unworthy players often admire them.)
基既处已，总投于地，以次行列，取而安之。（取球安于基内也。）	**Once the base has been set up, all the players should throw a ball along the ground and stand in queue according to the order. Players put their balls on the base with this order.** (Putting balls in the base area.)
远者先，近者后；左者先，右者后。（离窝远者先击，若头棒者，左边先击。）	**Long distance first and short distance second; left side first and right side second.** (Whose ball lands farthest from the hole plays first, while the player with a ball nearest the hole plays last. If these are the players' first strokes,[1] the player with the ball standing on the left side plays first.)

所以置先后之序也。（此乃定先后之法也。）	**These are the rules governing order of play**. (This is the method of determining the order of play.)

[1] In this case, the distances to the hole are the same.

试艺章第十	**Rule 10. Technical aspects of play**
权，（权者，所持之棒也，故以棒为操之权。）	**Qúan**, [1] (*Quan* is a club held by player. Therefore, the clubs are the power in players' hands.)
有立者，（揎当立而运，十数为全副，八数为中副，其次为小副。飞者、立者，次及十棒，不可改制。行者不可使飞，飞者不可使行。扑棒单手者，当立运者也。）	**The clubs for standing players**, (For playing from the upright position, use the *cuan* club, Ten clubs make a full set, there are eight in a middle set and fewer than eight constitute a small set. Clubs for air shots and for ground shots should not number more than ten, and this should not be changed. If a club is suitable for ground shot, it is not suitable for air shot. If a club is suitable for air shot, it is not suitable for ground shot. Players should stand when using a *pu* club for single arm strokes.)
蹲者，（今人曰减膝是也。杓棒鹰嘴当蹲。）	**The clubs for playing from a squatting position**, (Now this is called 'hitting with low knees'. *Shao* clubs, having a head shaped like an eagle-beak, should be used when the players are at low knees position.)
行者，（揎棒是也。）	**The clubs for ground shots**, (*Cuan* clubs are the correct ones.)
飞者，（扑棒，单手杓棒是也。）	**The clubs for air shots**, (*Pu* clubs and single-arm *shao* clubs are the right clubs.)
远者立，近者蹲。（随宜用力也。）	**If a player wants to make a long shot then an upright position is best, but for a short stroke it is better to adopt a position with bended knees.** (Adjust the strength of the swing according to the location of the ball.)
无阻则行，有阻则飞。（随宜用棒。）	**Make a ground shot when there is no obstruction, but if there is an obstruction, make an air shot.** (Choose a club appropriate to the situation.)
行者不蹲，（揎棒不减膝。）	**Players should not squat for a ground shot.** (When a *cuan* club is used, the player should not be in a squatting position.)
飞者随宜。（扑棒单手当立，杓棒鹰嘴当蹲。）	**Select a suitable club and player's position for air shots.** (If a single-arm *pu* club is used, the player should stand in a suitable position. With a *shao* club the player should be squatting.)
有阻不定行，无阻不定飞；有阻多飞，无阻多行。（随宜斟酌用棒，务在取中。）	**When there is an obstruction, do not always use a ground shot, and if there is no obstruction, do not always use an air shot. With an obstruction, often make air shots, and without an obstruction, often make ground shots.** (Select a suitable club and make sure the ball goes to the correct direction.)

返此则迷。（若执定一端，取中难矣。）	**A player ignoring this advice will get confused.** (If a player insists on using only one type of stroke, it is difficult to achieve any success.)
是以持欲固，（紧持棒也。）	**When holding, hold tightly.** (Hold the club tightly.)
运欲和，（使力得中。）	**When striking, make a smooth shot.** (The strength used should be moderate.)
无低昂，（不起身疾也。）	**Do not raise or lower the body during striking.** (Do not raise your body too fast.)
无空权。（二手皆当有棒也。空，去声。）	**Use the hands to hold the club.** (Both hands should hold club.)
心手相对，古之法也。（运棒时手对心。）	**Hold a club with two hands in a palm-to-palm position. This is the traditional way to hold clubs.** (When using a club, two hands should be in a palm-to-palm position.)

[1] 'Quan' originally means power. See also Rule 17. Here it means club.

记止章第十一	**Rule 11. Marking the position of the ball**
丸至之所，（球所在处也。）	**Where the ball lands,** (That is, where the ball has landed.)
当以杖画，（记其止也。）	**should be marked with a stick,** (This shows where the ball stops.)
勿前勿后，勿左勿远，（恐彼有所利也。）	**being not at the front nor the back, being not at the left nor far away from the ball.** (To avoid someone taking advantage from marking.)
唯画于右，可去寸许，长亦相比。（定法也。）	**A mark must be drawn on the right hand side of the ball, an inch away from the ball and an inch in length.** (This is the rule.)
凡动于我，（或球撞，或衣动，或足动，或手动，或棒动，或他物动球也。）	**If someone accidently moves my ball,** (by collision with a ball, or moved by clothes, foot, hand, club or other items.)
令安画首，（令彼动我球者，代我安于初所画之前头。）	**he must put it back to the front of the marked landing place,** (The person who moves my ball should put the ball back to the front of the original place.)
勿远勿后。（恐彼得利。）	**not far away from the marked line nor behind it.** (for avoiding people taking advantage.)

彼乃为败，（彼既动我球，彼球已击则不用，未击则不许击也。）	He then loses a stroke. (If he has already played a shot before moving his fellow player's ball, his last short does not count. If he has not played, he is not allow to strike in this turn.)
我若无画，彼虽为败，吾亦任去，不可复位。（若我初无画，彼动我球，则任我球之所往，不可取回复安本处。彼虽为输，恐我亦不得其利故也。）	If my ball's landing mark has not been drawn before it is moved by another player, the mover loses a stroke and the ball stays where ever it has stopped. It cannot be put back to its original place. (If I do not place a landing mark immediately and someone moves my ball, the ball must remain in its final position. It cannot be returned to its original position. Although the mover misses a stroke because of his action, I, regretfully, may not gain any advantage from this situation.)
相去分厘，（两球相离也。）	If two balls are about one inch or less apart, (That is to say the balls are separated.)
及有妨阻，（今人谓之圽子。）	and there is an obstruction nearby, (Nowadays, it is called a mound.)
无复动移，（两球相并，及有圽子，俱不可动。若动者，为输。）	both balls must not be moved to a more playable position. (If two balls are next to each other and there is a mound nearby, neither ball can be moved. Anyone moving a ball loses.)
中身为败，复从我击。（我球着他人身者，他人为败，取我之球再复击之，不击，亦从我心。）	If my ball hits someone, that person loses. I have the chance to repeat the shot if I wish. (If my ball hits someone, that person will lose. I can take my ball and strike again or choose not to do so, as I wish.)

制财章第十二	Rule 12. Contributing to prizes
富不出微财，(富厚者不吝啬。)	Wealthy people should not contribute only a small amount of money as prizes. (Wealthy people should not be too stingy.)
贫不出重货。(贫薄者不倍偿。)	The poor should not make over-generous donations of money and goods. (People who are poor should not make contributions worth twice what others give.)
富出微财则耻，贫出重货则竭。(量力而为之可也。)	It is shameful for a wealthy person to give small sums of money for prizes; poor people who make larger donations will suffer the effects of poverty. (Make a contribution according to your financial circumstances.)
智者有方财不绝，(捶击有法，故得常胜，所以财不尽也。)	Wise people have good playing techniques and frequently win money. (Because they play each stroke well, they often win and so regularly earn money.)
愚者无方将恐竭。(捶击无法，所以常负，财不足用也。)	In contrast, poor players have no good playing skills and eventually may lose all their money. (Such people, because of

	poor playing skills, often lose games and have not enough money for continuing the game.)
不绝者，必胜之基，(财不绝，则心安，故胜。)	**A good income is fundamental to success,** (Keeping money all the time results in a peaceful mind, a good basis for success.)
将竭者，必败之道。(财将尽，心不安，愈怯愈输也。)	**and a decline in wealth is a clear sign of failure.** (With a falling income the mind of the player becomes disturbed and, the more anxious they are, the less likely they are to win.)

衍数章第十三	**Rule 13. Scale of competition**
十数、九数为大会，八数、七数为中会，六数、五数为小会，四数、三数为一朋，二人为单对。十数、八数、六数可分，不分从之，九数、七数、五数、四数、三数皆不分。(双数可分，单数不可分。四数虽双，数少亦不可分也。)	**A game with ten or nine players is a large competition, eight or seven is medium, while six or five is small. Playing with four or three players is an individual event in a game called a** *Peng.* **Two players form a single pair. Ten, eight or six players can be divided into two teams or keep undivided as the players wish. Nine, seven, five, four, or three players cannot be divided into two teams.** (An even number of players can be divided into two teams but an odd number not so. Although four is an even number, there are too few players to make teams.)
分者，相朋也；(朋者，班也。)	**Separation of the players into teams is a process of looking for favourite team-mates.** (*Peng*, team-mates, means forming a group.)
不分者，各逞其能也。相朋者，一朋胜多为赢，(倘五人为一班，于一班中多胜一人者是赢，相等曰平。)	**When players are not divided into teams, they play individually with their own abilities. In team competitions, the team with the higher number of winning players wins in the final competition.** (For example, with teams of five players, the team which has the larger number of winning players wins the competition. If both teams have the same number of winning players, it is an equal.)
各逞者，他不胜而我胜为赢。(初棒赢二棒，二棒赢三棒，三棒赢四棒，是也。)	**In individual play, if another player does not hit the ball into the hole, but I do, then I win.** (A player who hits the ball into the hole in one stroke beats one using two strokes. A player with two strokes beats a player with three strokes and a player using three strokes beats a player using four. This is what the text means.)
于三会中，(大会、中会、小会。)	**In all three types of competitions,** (the large, medium and small competitions,)
俱胜一败，免一败者，(俱上，独一不上，免一不上者。)	**if all players in the same team but one win then the loser does not have to contribute to the prize money.** (When it is a team competition, all players but one in the same team win their

	matches, the one who does not win is exempt from making a contribution to the prize money.)
一朋一败，勿免其取。(三四人击丸，独一不上，不可不取其物，数少故也。)	**However, if there is one player in a *peng* who loses, this loser's contribution to the prize money cannot be waived.** (When three or four players play as a group in a competition, and only one loses, a contribution to the prizes from this loser has to be collected, because of the number of players is too small.)
一日不三会，(一日不赌三会，惜物故也。)	**People must not participate in three or more games in a day.** (Players should not participate in three or more competitions in the same day as contributing to the prize money is expensive.)
有遗不为输，(二十筹为满，倘赢得十九筹，是遗一筹。若遗一筹，利物不可得矣。)	**Even if the required number of playing tokens is not attained, the game is not a failure.** (To win a large competition twenty playing tokens are required. If a team obtains only 19, it is one short of the winning number and cannot claim any prizes.)
昨所得，今不用，义也。(昨日胜得十九筹，唯一筹未得，今日不可理昨日所胜十九筹，乃义聚之道也。)	**Playing tokens won yesterday are not used for today. It is chivalrous.** (If a team won 19 playing tokens yesterday, only one token short of the winning number, these tokens are not used in today's match. This is to make the game more ethical.)

运筹章第十四	**Rule 14. Counting tokens**
大筹二十，中筹十五，小筹一十。(此谓分班，时三会也。)	**Twenty tokens are needed in a big match, fifteen in a medium one and only ten in a small match.** (These are the three categories for competitions in which players are divided into teams.)
初胜三，次胜二，后胜一。(牌数。)	**Holing the ball with one stroke gets three tokens, with two strokes gets two tokens and three strokes gets only one.** (This is the number of tokens awarded.)
初胜次，次胜后，后胜四。(初赢二，二赢三，三赢四。)	**The first beats the second, the second beats the third, which beats the fourth.** (Holing with the first stroke wins against two strokes, holing with two strokes wins against three strokes, which wins against four strokes.)
四者不可用也。(不可打第四棒。)	**A fourth stroke does not result in the award of a token.** (It is not necessary to play the fourth stroke.)
最上多初，其中多次，其下多后。(上、中、下之能也。)	**The best players often hole in one stroke, the modest players generally achieve this with a second stroke, but the poor players often hole with the third stroke.** (This refers to playing ability, top, middle and low.)

复有争先，满三竭五。（每人五牌，三番胜，方得一牌。如此五番，他牌尽。）	**If a further competition is needed between two, completing three holings for one token and losing five tokens ends the game.** (Each player begins with five tokens and, after winning three holings, the player wins one token. When a player loses all five tokens, he loses the game.)
胜得一，（所谓初棒、二棒、三棒都同，止得一牌。）	**Every winning earns one token,** (Holing with the first, second and third strokes are the same. All wins only one token.)
无再争。（一人上窝，余皆不用。）	**no double holing.** (If one player has already hit the ball into a hole there is no further play at that hole.)
上者不偏能，（飞行远近，不偏能一种也。）	**The best players should not have just one skill.** (For long or short distance shots, they should not only be good at one skill.)
中者亚之，（比上者稍低，亦不偏能也。）	**Modest players are less skilful,** (Their skills are lower than the best players, but they should also cultivate more than one skill.)
下者阻其偏，不可行矣。（下等者，若不随意，则必窘矣。）	**Poor players do not win because their limited skill, so they cannot play well.** (When the poor players face some unexpected conditions, they often do not know how to deal with them.)
是故必擅可也。（欲专此事，必精此艺。）	**Therefore, one must be an expert.** (If you want to be a professional player, you must obtain excellent skills.)

决胜章第十五	**Rule 15. How to win the game**
众为己败之形，（己败之形者，失棒、换棒、着身、着球、悬空挂窝、砖上阁球、淤持基、拿死球、踏圴子、放圴子、那球、踢人球儿、换死球基中、模圴子、上棒球儿、自上画、数次安球、基中试棒、基外安球、画基不于左、堘上行。）	**These are signs of losing the games,** (For example, throwing away the club, changing the club, being hit by other player's ball, touching another player's ball, passing over the hole with a club to sweep the ball into the hole, putting a brick underneath the ball, making the starting base more solid, moving your ball away from a 'dead' position, treading a mound, building a mound, moving the ball, kicking away another player's ball, returning the ball that has landed in an unfavourable place back to the starting base, making a mound-like obstacle, hitting the ball with the wooden part of a club, drawing player's own landing marks, making several attempts to place a ball on starting base, practising strokes on a base, placing a ball outside a base, not standing on the left hand side to draw a base, walking on the pathway of playing fields, etc.)
吾为决胜之妙。（得之于心，应之于手，志过于人，是为决胜。）	**which leave me wonderful chances to win.** (My aspirations are from my heart. My ability to accomplish these aspirations is in my hand. My ambition is greater than that of others. These are the determinants of victory.)
人皆见我所以中之能，而莫知吾所以制胜之能，（机深识广，人难度也。）	**People only see my skilful performances, but they don't know why I can win and my real ability at winning,** (I have extensive knowledge and clever strategies about how to play, which are not easily understood by others.)

妙之妙者也。	that is the value of a lucky break.
风坠而中，不可为胜，若不隔墒，[1] 可准初中。（风吹上窝者，别人已安球在基内，则不算初棒，未曾安球在基者，算初棒。）	When wind blows a ball into the hole, this cannot be regarded as an ideal case. However, if it happens before the next player starts to strike, then it counts as holing with the first stroke. (When wind blows a ball into the hole after another player has already placed a ball on the base, it does not count as a first-stroke winning. However, if it happens before placing the ball on the base, it counts as a first-stroke winning.)
抑亦乘机决胜之妙也。（此在己之能虑胜而后会，亦兵家之成算也。）	Using the wind is a wonderful strategy of taking advantage of a good chance. (This is because it is planned carefully in advance to achieve victory, which is also used in military schemes to win battles.)
[1], '墒' here is probably a typo and should be '轮', meaning 'run'.	

出奇章第十六	Rule 16. Surprised play
致于死地则无生，致于生地则无怯。死而复生，生而复死，谓之出奇。（心手相应故也。）	When a ball lands in an unfavourable or 'dead' place, it is impossible to play further. When the ball is in a favourable place, the player will be confident. A 'dead' ball is suddenly rescued. A favourable ball is hit to a 'dead' place. These are called surprised plays. (Surprised play reflects the ability of the player to use his skill to match the strategy required.)
君子无所怯，小人有所惧。无怯者坦然，有惧者戚然。坦则多胜，戚则多败。多胜者神舒而气和，多败者色厉而内荏。（人心有所主，则无惧无怯，量胜而击之，故无败衄；心无所主，则妄动而失利。将之用兵亦然。）	Worthy people have confidence and do not fear to play, but unworthy people have no confidence and are fearful. People without fears are calm and peaceful, whereas those with fears are worried and angry. The former often win whereas people who are worried and angry often lose. The players who often win are usually gentle and polite to other people as they are relaxed and pleasant. The players who often lose usually appear to be superficially strong, but are weak in heart. (When players have strategies and are confident, they have no fears during the game. They take any opportunity to beat others and hardly ever fail. If a player has no strategy or confidence he may take reckless actions. As a result he loses the advantage. In war, a general in command of his troops uses the same principle.)
智者察之，迫而胜之，（彼既怯，可急乘机而胜之。）	Wise people can see the opportunities and so press on with their strategies to win the game, (Because the opponents have already lost their confidence, wise people can quickly seize the opportunity and win.)

若陨大石于高山矣。（彼既怯而败，我既陵而胜，则我之势如高山推球，不可阻矣，良将以之。）	**as a rock falling from a mountain cannot be stopped.** (Our opponents lose the game because of their fears but we win because we are strong. Our strength is like the force of a rock falling down a mountain. It is too powerful to be stopped. Good generals act like that.)

丸经下卷 （凡十六章）	***Wan Jing* Vol 2**
权舆章第十七	**Rule 17. Making Clubs and Balls**
权舆，始计也。造衡自权始，造车自舆始。丸准轮，轮量权，权量身。（球欲量棒大小，棒欲量身长短，相称则利，相欺则不利矣。）	*Qúan yù* [1] is the starting point of strategy. To make a steelyard, it starts from a counterweight. To make a carriage, it starts from the carriage body. The balls should match the template ring, the ring size depends on the length of clubs, and the length of clubs should suit a player's height. (To make *chui wan* balls, the length of clubs should be measured first.To make clubs, the height of the player should be considered. It is beneficial if all these measurements are matched and a disadvantage if they are not.)
琢磨之失，虽能亦败。（造棒刮棒，失其法度，虽善击者，亦不能以巧胜彼矣。）	**If clubs are not cut and polished properly, even skilled players will lose matches.** (If the standards of making and polishing clubs are not followed, even the players, who can make very good shots, cannot beat their opponents with their excellent skills.)
突者宽薄，遥者窄厚。（突者，激起也，而欲皮面宽，木分薄；遥者，击远也，凡扑棒、撺棒、单手杓棒，欲令致远，必须皮面窄，木分厚。若违此式，则不相应矣。）	**Clubs for short pitch shots should be wide and thin and for long air shots should be narrow and thick.** (Short pitch shots allow the balls to jump for a short distance. For such shots the leather part of the club head should be wide and the wooden part should be thin. Long air shots mean balls are stroke to a long distance. The appropriate clubs are '*pu* club', '*cuan club*', and single-hand '*shao club*'. [2] To make a long shot, the leather part of the club head must be narrow and the wooden part should be thick. If these regulations are not followed, the goals cannot be achieved.)
偏欹为乖，（棒头不可拽手，不可脱手。）	**Skewed grips are not good.** (The end of the club, i.e. the grips, should not drag the hands, nor escape from the hands.)
端为中，（棒头中为妙。）	**The grip should be in line with the centre of the shaft.** (It is excellent if the grip of a club is in line with the centre of the shaft.)
不预磨削，（不预磨削，恐翘坏矣。）	**The sticks for making clubs should not be cut too much in advance,** (Not cutting too early is to avoid possible damage of the shaft and bend later.)
不毁心脊，（勿将棒中心刮陷，及将脊刮低也。）	**Do not damage the centre or ridge of the stick.** (Do not over scrape the centre of the wood stick to avoid causing concavity.)

先刃次脊，后平其心。（最后刮心也。）	Remove the branches in the stick first and then cut the central part. (Cutting the central part of the stick last.)
赘木为丸，乃坚乃久。（赘木者，瘿木也。瘿木坚牢，故可久而不坏。）	Use superfluous wood to make balls that are hard and will last for a long time. (The Superfluous wood is gall wood, which is hard and therefore can be used without damage for a long time.)
无窦为劣，轻重欲称。（无眼者不可用，太重则迟，太轻则飘。）	The balls without pores on the surface are poor. The weight of the balls should be appropriate. (Do not use wood without small holes for the balls. If the wood used for the balls is too heavy then the speed of the balls is reduced. If the wood is too light the balls would float.)
工从主，料以理，（工者，匠也。造棒必从击球主人心之所好，凡治料诸棒，必当依此理也。）	Club makers should obey their custmers, including selection of the materials. (Club makers are craftsmen. When making clubs the craftsman must do what their custmers want and like. The same principle applies in selection of the materials for clubs.)
善胜者，不恃力，唯恃地。（知地形为上。）	Success in winning matches does not depend on strength, but on the knowledge of ground conditions of the playing area. (Knowing the land topography in the playing area is the most important thing for success.)

[1] 'Quan' is a counterweight for steelyard balance and 'yù' is the main body of a carriage. 'Quan yu' is a term, meaning a start point. 'Quan' also means power and club, see Rule 10.
[2] Different clubs have different functions. For example, 'pu club' is for striking, 'cuan club' is for fling, and single-hand 'shao club' is for rolling. Also see Rule 4.

制器章第十八	Rule 18 Making implements
工欲善其事，必先利其器。（夫欲精善其艺，必须得好利器。谓如击得球好，亦须得好棒。）	For craftsmen to make quality products they must have good tools. (To achieve an excellent craftsmanship, one must have very good tools. This is the same principle in playing *chui wan*. If players wish to perform well in playing *chui wan*, they must have good clubs.)
器利艺精，心手相应，临事发机，无不中也。（又有好棒，丸经之妙，悟之于心，捶击之法,熟之于手，百发百中。今有新旧权制，具录于左。）	With good equipment and perfect technique, If players are able to adapt their technical skills to match their strategies, when they have opportunities to win in games, they will not miss a single target. (If players have good clubs, understand well the wonderful theory described in '*Wan Jing*', have perfect grip for striking, they will always get the targets without a single miss. Nowadays, there are both new and old ways of making clubs for specific hitting, which are all recorded on the left hand side. [1])
正棒头打八面，倒棒斜插花，	'*Zheng*' club head with all around surface treated,'*dao*' club with '*slanting flower*', [2]
卧棒斜插花，揣棒斜插花，	'*wo*' club with '*slanting flower*', '*chuan*' club with '*slanting flower*', [3]

皮塔斜插花，燕尾斜插花，	'*pi ta*' with '*slanting flower*', '*swallowtail*' with '*slanting flower*', [4]
倒棒翻卷帘，底板基儿，	'*dao*' club with a shape like '*turning over rolling curtain*', supporting layer on the substrate board,
脥里基儿，两肩基儿，	supporting layer underneath the faces, supporting layer on the two shoulders,
山口四面基儿，山口四面打皮塔，	supporting layer on four sides of '*shan-kou*', [5] feather layer is applied on four sides of '*shan-kou*',
山口打棒尾，背身打土儿，	'*Shan-kou*' at club end, turning around to hit soil, [6]
背身打翻杖，背身弹棒，	turning around to play '*fan*' club, turning around using '*Tan*' club, [7]
背身正棒，背身扑棒，	turning around to play '*zheng*' club, turning around to play '*pu*' club,
竹撅儿打四边，皮塔打八面，	up turned bamboo piece on 4 sides, feather piece on all 8 faces,
近双弹棒，远双弹棒，	double '*tan*' club for short distance, double '*tan*' club for long distance, [8]
三根弹棒，叠柄弹棒，	three-root '*tan*' clubs, overlapped stems '*tan*' club,
三撅三球弹棒，双撅双球倒棒打撺，	triple up-turn and triple beads '*tan*' club, double up-turn and double beads '*dao*' club for '*cuan*' stroke, [9]
井里拔，正棒头翻撅儿，	'*Pulling-from-well*', '*zheng*' club head with up-turn, [10]
棒尾皮塔， 棒尾打四边，	club end with feather piece, club end with treatment on 4 sides,
棒上安偏棒，棒上安正棒，	tilted club join to another club, '*zheng*' club join to another club,
棍儿飐棒，前撅翻过后，	stick with '*zhan*' club, [11] up-turn in front turning to back,
后撅掀过前，棍子翻撅儿，	up-turn on back turning to front, stick with pouty lips,
杓儿翻撅儿（已上新法。）	'*shao*' club head with pouty lips. (The above are listed in the new methods.)
土尖，砖角，球上球，	*mound-tip, brick-corner*, ball on ball,

翻杖，直杖，纽杖，	turnover stick, straight stick, spiral stick,
靴尖，雁点头，泥撅儿，	tip of boots, *nod of a wild-goose*, mud up-turn, [12]
泥虾蟆，正棒头，倒棒头，	*mud toad*, '*zheng*' club head, '*dao*' club head,
土尖棒尾，飐棒，积棒，	*Mound-tip* club end, '*zhan*' club, '*ji*' club, [13]
打燕尾，远近小土儿（已上古法。）	making a swallowtail, small mound shape for long and short strokes. (The above are listed in the old methods.)

[1] 'On the left hand side' here means 'as following', because traditionally, Chinese was written in vertical columns from top to bottom; the first column being on the right side of the page, and the last column on the left. The list below of methods of making clubs, 37 new methods and 17 old ones, gives only names without further descriptions. Therefore, it is very difficult to guess the details.

[2] '*Zheng*' and '*dao*' have opposite meaning. '*Zheng*' means upright and '*dao*' means upside down. These seem to describe different club heads. '*Slanting flower*' probably means special patterns on clubs.

[3] '*Wo*' means lying down. '*Wo*' club is a type of club.

[4] '*Pi*' means feather and '*ta*' means column. Both '*pi ta*' and '*swallowtail*' are parts of clubs.

[5] '*Shan-kou*' seems to be a shape on the surface of club, but its location is not determined. '*Shan*' means hill and '*kou*' means mouth. The original meaning of '*shan-kou*' is a location between two adjacent hills. It is also used to describe the holes on a flute or the stands for strings in some Chinese stringed instruments, such as 'lute' or 'Banjo'.

[6] Not sure whether the meaning of this sentence is correct. '*Tu*' means soil or land. However, it can also mean chalk.

[7] '*Fan*' means turning over. Playing '*fan*' club is more likely a style of play rather than a type of club. '*Tan*' means jump or spring. '*Tan*' club may be for short but fast strokes.

[8] '*Tan*' clubs are one type of clubs. '*Tan*' means 'pop up'.

[9] '*Cuan*' stroke means stroke by '*cuan*' club. The original meaning of '*cuan*' is to throw. Therefore, '*cuan*' in the game means air shot.

[10] '*Pulling-from-well*' probably means hitting a ball from a concave ground.

[11] '*Zhan*' means shaking in wind. Here 'zhan' club is a kind of design for club.

[12] These are three different designs of club heads.

[13] '*Ji*' means accumulate or old. Here '*ji*' club is a type of club.

取材章第十九	**Rule 19 Selecting materials**
取材之方，不可不察。（夫欲造棒，采取材料，不可不知其法。）	**The method of selecting materials should not be ignored.** (To make clubs, one must know the method of choosing materials.)
秋冬取木，用其坚也。（秋冬木植，津气在内，所以坚牢，故可取也。）	**Timber should be taken in the autumn and winter, because they are harder in these seasons.** (Plants in the autumn and winter maintain nutritional fluids and vital energy inside their bodies, therefore, they are harder and more tenacious. Thus, they can be taken for use.)
筋胶以牛，用其固也。（牛筋牛胶，性最坚固，其他不及也。）	**The glue should be made from the tendons and skin of cattle due to their high strength.** (The tendons and skin of cattle are the strongest compared with others.)

竹取劲干，用其刚也。（南方大竹，刚劲厚实，故可为柄。）	**Use strong trunks of bamboo for their hardness.** (Huge bamboos from the South are thicker and harder, so they can be used for making stems of clubs.)
朴斲以时，用其柔也。（春夏天气温暖，筋胶相和，可以造棒也。）	**Making clubs from the raw materials should be undertaken in a good season when the weather is mild.** (The warmth of the weather in spring and summer allows glue to stick well with wood. That is the time to make clubs.)

适宜章第二十	**Rule 20. Selecting the appropriate distance**
远近随宜，（或远或近，随人便也，）	**A suitable distance between the starting place and the hole is chosen by the players.** (Long or short distance, it can be chosen by the players and should reflect their ability.)
各安其能。（随各人所能，用棒索窝。）	**The distance should reflect an individual's ability.** (This depends on the player's ability in using their clubs to hole the balls.)
远无百步之遥，（虽远勿出百步之外。）	**A long distance should not be more than 100 footsteps.** (The long distance must not be any longer than 100 footsteps.)
近必盈丈之外。（一丈之内太近，故必一丈之外，以及数丈之类也。）	**A short distance must be more than one 'zhang'.** [1] (Less than one 'zhang' will be too close to the hole. Therefore, it must be more than one zhang, or even be a few zhangs away.)
远多则疲，（运力多，故疲。）	**Too many long shots will make players tired.** (More strength is needed to play long shots and players may become too tired.)
近多则弱。（不能致远，故弱。）	**On the other hand, choosing short strike too often indicates the weakness of the players.** (Because players are unable to make long distance shots, they must be weak.)
远者难从，近者易行。（致远者少，致近者多。）	**Holing the ball with a long shot is more difficult than using a short shot.** (This means that fewer people play long shots and more people play short shots.)
有力者利远，无力者利近。（强弱不同。）	**Strong people like to play long shots and weak people prefer short shots.** (This is because the difference in strength.)
远者拙，（粗也。）	**Playing a long shot requires a powerful swing,** (Coarse action.)
近者巧。（细也。）	**whilst a short shot requires greater skill.** (Fine action.)
百步之遥不可再，（太远不可两遭。）	**Players should not attempt a '100-footstep' shot more than once in a game.** (Since it is too far away, the players should not do it twice.)

| 半百之遥不可数。（五六十步不可频数。） | **Players should not play too many times with distances about a half of hundred footsteps.** (The players should not play too frequently for shots for 50 or 60 footsteps.) |
| 各适其宜而已矣。（远近适其宜而已矣。） | **All individual players should choose their appropriate ways to play.** (Selection of distance depends on which is more suitable to them.) |

[1] '*Zhang*' is a length unit used in China. One '*zhang*' is about three metres. The distance of one hundred footsteps is about 40 metres.

处用章第二十一	**Rule 21. Regulations during play**
熟地必革，（谓熟窝不再击，每日须当改革。）	**The playing area must be changed.** (Players must not choose holes with which they are familiar, so the course must be changed daily.)
毋教以利，（不许指与人地形埒道便利处，教者算输。）	**Players must not tell others how to play best on a particular course.** (It is not permitted to point out to other players how to best use the terrain to advantage. If you do, then you lose.)
阻利不许，（不许放均子及埇土，脚躐陷地，如此者算输。）	**You must not prevent, in any way, others scoring points.** (Players must not make obstructions, build mud barriers or use their feet to make a concavity on the ground in the pathway to the hole. If you do so, you lose.)
假权勿从，（不许借棒与他人使。）	**You must not allow other players to use your clubs.** (You must not lend your clubs to other players.)
错丸弃之。（错击他人球者算输。）	**Do not hit a wrong ball.** (The player who hits other player's ball will lose.)
为妨出之，（或前或后、或左或右，影他人使棒，如此者出之。）	**Obstructing other players will result in disqualification.** (Any player interfering with another player's swing at the front, back, to the left or to the right, is out of the game.)
阴结为奸，（谓二人平日相亲爱，或分班时分开，而于自班中故不肯用意，以致失利。如此乃谓暗中与人相结，是为朋奸。如此者，勿使分开。若彼二人自欲分开而复如此者，名曰打劫，不可以入会矣。）	**Undercover joint to be liaison.** (For example, two very close friends are separated into two teams. One does not play to his full ability so his team loses. That means this player is in an undercover collaboration with another player in the opposing team, the so-called conspiracy. In this case, these two players should not be allowed to play in opposing teams. If both of them request to be in opposing teams and repeatedly do so, then it is called a 'robbery' and they should not be allowed to play.)
非击为败，（挑、拨、推、砍、兜、削、刮、舀、扫、碾，如此者，皆算输。）	**Hitting the ball improperly results in a loss.** (Examples are picking, poking, pushing, chopping, scooping, chipping, scraping, spooning, sweeping and grinding and so on, which all result in loss.)

代施倍罚。（替他人击者，算输二塯。）	**Substituting for another player should get double punishments.** (If you stand in to play for another player, you will be penalised by losing two rounds.)
驭众处用之道也。（亦兵家鞠旅用卒之义也。）	**The above principles govern the game and players' conduct.** (These principles are similar to the way to use military forces in army.)

观形章第二十二	**Rule 22. Observation of the terrain of playing area**
击不他视，专睹其丸；他视伤权，专睹必利。(夫击球时，眼勿看窝而下棒，专观于球，必得其利。)	A player should give his full attention to the ball when playing it. Do not glance around as you do so. Clubs can be damaged if you mis-hit the ball because of a lack of focus. Concentration aids good play. (When a player hits the ball his eyes should not be on the hole he is aiming for but on the ball. Looking at the ball will give him an advantage.)
权从心，（棒随心转。）	**The club follows the mind,** (The movement of the club should follow the player's thoughts.)
心从形。（心从地势。）	**and the thoughts reflect the terrain.** (The player's thoughts should reflect the terrain of the playing area.)
从心先形，（欲从心所作，必先观其地形。）	**To follow the thoughts, observe the terrain first.** (If the player intends to play with his thoughts, he must first observe the terrain.)
从形必中，（随地形者必上窝。）	**Following the terrain leads into hole.** (Players who play games according to the terrain of the playing ground will certainly hit balls into holes.)
从形者胜，从力者败。（随地形者胜，恃自力者败。）	**If you carefully consider the terrain you will win. If you rely solely on strength you will fail.** (Player who comply with the terrain of the play ground will win and those who depend on their strength will lose.)
从力虽胜，谓之侥幸。（偶然得也。）	**Although players who play with their strength may sometimes win the game, they win by luck.** (This only happens occasionally.)

善行章第二十三	**Rule 23. Behaviour while playing** [1]
行止者，嫌爱之端，（行止善则可敬，不善则可鄙厌；）	**People decide to like or hate you according to your conduct and manners.** (People with good behaviour and manners are respected but bad behaviour and manners make you disliked.)

言语者，荣辱之阶。（言不可妄诞，妄诞则辱，不妄则荣。）	**How one speaks forms steps to glory or disgrace.** (Do not speak presumptuously or exaggerate as both are despicable. If you avoid both you will be glorious.)
讷于言，敏于行，正己践言，是为善行。（慎言语，谨行止，先行其言，斯为善矣。）	**Talking little, acting promptly and fulfilling what you say are all signs of good behaviour.** (Speaking cautiously, acting carefully and doing what you promised are all signs of good behaviour.)
言行有常，君子贵之。（言顾行，行顾言，成德人也。）	**Disciplined speaking and behaviour are valuable characteristics of a gentleman.** (What you say and what you do should be consistent. Players with high morals let their actions reflect their words.)
[1] This rule has little direct relevance to *chui wan* but describes the behaviour of a Confucian gentleman in all his activities.	

宁志章第二十四	**Rule 24. Following own ambition**
心之所之，定而处之，勿徇于己。（心所定向，无循己私。）	**Following your ambition, do according to your targeted achievement. You must not practice favoritism.** (When you have ambition, follow it. Do not vie for small benefit.) [1]
赧莫赧于易，（易者，将本色球儿相换，及球儿在不好处换在好处。）	**Nothing is more shameful than changing balls.** (Changing balls means the player replaces his ball, which has landed in a difficult place, by another ball of the same colour at a better place.)
耻莫耻于复。（复者，初击不利，欲再击也。）	**Nothing is more humiliating than hitting repeatedly.** (Hitting repeatedly means, when the first hit is not favourable, the player intends to hit it again.)
既易既复，同朋尽败。（若易球，若重击，非但本人为输，同班尽皆作输。虽曾得胜，亦不为胜。）	**By changing a ball or hitting a ball repeatedly, all players in that team will lose.** (If a player changes a ball, or hits a ball repeatedly, not only the player will lose, but all members of the team will lose. Even if they won the previous rounds, they still not win the game.)
悬有三，曰高，曰平，曰低，不可用也。（高者，仰也；平者，立也；低者，盈寸而下空也。悬球于此三者，皆不可用也。）	**There are three kinds of suspended balls, namely high, level and low locations. Balls at these positions cannot be further played.** (The high location means that people have to look up to see them, the level location is when the ball is at a level similar to the player's height, and the low location is when the ball is overhang at a position more than one inch above the ground. Balls that are in these three locations cannot be played any further.)
[1] '私' here means small.	

集智章第二十五	**Rule 25 Accumulating wisdom**
善巧者不以力，（不恃力也。）	**Skilled players do not rely on strength.** (They do not merely rely on their strength.)

善争者不以奇。（善争者，君子之争，君子不作奇怪也。）	**Players who are good at competitions do not use any odd techniques.** (Players who are good at competitions play the game with a noble manner and gentlemen do not use any strange techniques.)
善巧者左右逢其源，善争者嘿嘿而取胜。（艺高，不言而胜也。）	**Skilled players are able to achieve success one way or the other. Players who are good at competitions often win games while smiling.** (Skilled players win games in silence.)
奇怪索隐谓之侮，平易无颇谓之德。（平易可为法，奇怪不可学。）	**It is to bully and tease if you seek eccentric and sneaky ways to play. It is virtuous to use normal and decent ways to play.** (Normal and standard ways of playing can be regarded as rules. Players must not learn eccentric ways to play.)
奇怪者，人所未睹也；平易者，众所共知也。奇怪数出，君子疾之，小人玩之。（奇怪者，小人之所以争能也；平易者，君子之所以存心也。）	**The eccentric ways of play are those people have never seen. The so-called normal and decent ways are those people are familiar with. If a player often uses eccentric ways, he will be abhorred by worthy players, but welcomed by unworthy players.** (The eccentric ways are used by the unworthy players who strive to win. The standard ways are used by worthy players to show their sportsmanship.)

举要章第二十六	**Rule 26. Highlights**
众集纭纭，吾将傍通。（若众球聚在窝边，吾取地势傍通行之。傍通者，借墒也。）	**When there are many balls gathered near the hole, I will use a bypass.** (If many balls gather around the hole, I will take a bypass to *hit my ball to the hole* according to the local terrain. The bypass means using another pathway.)
鼎足难通，勇者必胜。（谓三人球在我前，一球正对，两球在正对之左右。吾欲左则左有阻，吾欲右则右有阻，欲正则正有阻，是以直至窝中必胜，勇者不怯也。）	**It is difficult to get pass a situation if there are balls located at three legs of a tripod cauldron on the way. However, brave players certainly will win.** (That is to say there are three balls of other players in front of the player. One is just at a position between the player and the hole. The other two are on the left and right. If the player tries to hit the ball to the left, there is a ball blocking the way. If the player wants to hit the ball to the right, there is a ball blocking the way as well. If the player intends to hit the ball straight ahead, there is also a ball getting in the way. Shotting the ball directly to the hole will win. Brave people are not afraid.) [1]
有强力之中，有势末之巧。（难至之所用力多，复有不须用力，但稍击，可随形上窝者。）	**Sometimes powerful strength is used for hitting balls into holes, whereas other times skillful hitting with weak force will do.** (When the ball is far away, hitting with a strength may be applied. In some other situations, no full force is needed. The player only needs to play with tiny force to get the ball into the hole because of correct use of the terrain.)
有不虞之中，（偶然中也。）	**Occasionally the player does not expect to hole the ball, but achieves it,** (Hitting a ball into the hole accidentally.)

有求中之蹶。（用诈求中，反成败蹶。）	In other cases, the player desperately wishes to hole, but **cannot achieve it.** (Trying hard for winning, some players even cheat during the games, but they still fail.) [2]
故先度为上，（先看地势，土性，度其远近，避其妨阻也。）	**Therefore, the best way is to have a careful investigation before playing.** (Before hitting, the players should observe the terrain and the characteristics of the earth, estimate the distance, and try to avoid obstructions.)
先度后动，百发百中；先动后度，百发百蹶。（不可侥幸求中，不度而中，谓之偶然。）	**Playing after investigation, the player always wins. Hitting before investigation, the player always loses.** (You must not expect to win games by luck. Holing without taking investigation is regarded as an accidental case.)
故曰；差之毫厘，失之千里。（分毫不可苟且。）	**There is an old saying that the least bit of discrepancy at the beginning may lead to a thousand miles of difference at the end.** (There is nothing you should be careless about.)
此决胜之要，智者所守也。（有智之人，必须熟览此书。）	**These are vital things to do to win games and wise people comply.** (Smart people should repeatedly read and get familiar with this book.)

[1] The original text means in a difficult situation with some balls blocking the way, the payer with confidence will win. The condition is that other balls must not be touched.
[2] The original text does not mention about cheating.

知几章第二十七	**Rule 27 Recognising motivation and opportunities**[1]
先人者制人，（捶击熟闲，心有定向，必能制人。）	**Leading players will overpower others.** (Players who are adept at hitting balls and have steady mind will most certainly overpower the others.)
后人者制于人。（捶击不就，熟临时发，志先怯弱，必为人所制也。）	**Players who are behind in the competition will be overpowered by others.** (Players who are less skilled at hitting balls have to rely on luck. Because their mind is preoccupied by fear, they will most certainly be overpowered by other players.)
制人者，人皆仰之；（心手相应，发无不中，人必称善。）	**The players who can overpower others are respected by all people.** (They are able to adapt their technical skills to suit their strategies. As a consequence, no hit misses its target. People will certainly praise them.)
制于人者，人皆卑之。（多死少活，人皆笑之。）	**The players who are overpowered by other players are despised by all people.** (They lose more games than they win, so people will laugh at them.)
人仰之，三军之帅也，（众心服而归之，将之用兵，亦由是也。）	**The players respected by people just like a commander-in-chief of all the three military forces.** [2] (People admire and follow them. The principle is the same as how a general uses military forces.)

人卑之，匹夫之谅也。（众所不与，难力争矣。）	**The players despised by others are really ordinary people with inflated ideas.** (People do not want to team-up with them, so they hardly win the games.)
几者，动之由，事之微，（几者，必心念发动之初，善恶从此而分，荣辱存焉。）	**Motivation is what causes people to act and also means traces of what is happening or is going to happen,** (Motivation must be built up at the initial stage when people start to act, which is the initial starting point, where good and bad behaviours of the players are separated. The players receive their honours or dishonours, accordingly.)
胜负之先见者也。（胜负皆萌于此。）	**Motivation also determines winning or losing games.** (Winning or losing the games originates from this point.)
知几知微，君子哉。（见几而作，不俟终日，惟君子能之。）	**Players who can recognise opportunities and identify tiny omens are worthy people.** (Crabbing the opportunities and acting without waiting for the whole day, that is what only the worthy people are able to achieve.)

[1] In ancient literature, '几 Ji' can have a meaning of omen or symptom of a trend. It can also be the same as '机 Ji', which means opportunity.
[2] In the *Chun-Qiu* period, the authorized strength of state army was structured by three large military units. However, one may consider that 'three' here means all military forces or several military units.

守中章第二十八	**Rule 28. Maintaining successful play**
击高当踰，致远当臻。（过树过墙，必当高超而过。击远者，必当所限。）	**When an air shot is required, the ball should be struck hard enough that it passes over the obstruction. Long shots should be powerful enough to reach the target.** (When trying to hit the ball over a tree or a wall, players must use a stroke such that the ball passes over them. A long shot must go far enough to reach the target.)
不踰不臻，为败之名。（不能过，不能制，为败。）	**If balls cannot pass over obstructions or reach the targets, then these shots are failures.** (If the shot is not high enough or does not go far enough, the shot is a failure.)
所操从人，（所操之棒，各从人心。）	**A player has control over his performance.** (How to use clubs depends on what individual player intends to do.)
所主从胜。（索窝从赢者。）	**It is important that a player's concern should be focused on winning games,** (That means to hit balls into holes in order to win the games.)
操不从人，主不从胜，君子不为也。（君子之人，不作此也。）	To play a game where **playing performances are uncontrollable and winning the game is not the players' abition, is not behaviour of worthy people.** (Worthy people will never behave like these.) ·

玩心章第二十九	Rule 29. The mental game [1]
斯术无方，制心为上；（收其放心也。）[2]	**The techniques are various, but nothing is more important than getting the players in the right state of mind.** (Constraining your indulgent mind.)
心体既明，玩心为上。（自己心体己明，必观他人之心如何。）	**Once a player is feeling physically and mentally relaxed, the important thing is to observe other players' psychological state.** (Once you are certain you are relaxed in mind and body, it is time to observe the mental state of your opponents.)
玩心者，观其形，听其声。有怯于心，必显诸形。显诸形者，我得迫而胜之。（睹形乘胜。）	**To investigate the mental states of others, the player should observe their expressions, body appearance, and listen to their tone of voice. If they have fear in mind, it will be certainly reflected in their stance. Whenever an opponent shows signs of fear, I should take it as a chance to win.** (Seeing the signs, act quickly and go forward to victory.)
怯者无复，（怯而输者，必难复胜。）	**The players with fears will not be able to turn the tables.** (If a player has played badly because of fear, it is difficult for him to win.)
既无以复，我可纵横。（纵横者，自在乘胜。）	**If the opponents have no chance to recover from previous defeats, I can play freely in all possible ways.** (That means I can play the game comfortably right through to a victory.)
纵之横之，彼心愈惊，彼惊我宁，必胜之征。（彼既惶惧，我心既安，必胜之道也。）	**Playing vertically and horizontally, the opponent would be getting more panic. While he is in a state of panic, I remain calm. These are signs of my certain victory.** (While the opponent is already scared, my mind is in peace, which is the way to a certain win.)
初胜勿骄，骄而必失。（初既胜，当自慎，毋为骄，骄必败。）	**If you are winning from an early stage, you must not become conceited. Conceit will definitely lead to failure.** (When you win at the beginning, you should become cautious, do not to be conceited, as conceit will certainly result in losing in the end.)
慎终如始，乃可无敌。（后比初愈谨，必胜无敌。）	**If you remain cautious from beginning to end, you can become unbeatable.** (If you can take more caution in the later stages of the game, then, certainly no one can beat you.)

[1] '玩心'. '玩' means 'to play' or ' to make fun of'; '心' means 'mind'. Therefore, the mind here is other people's mind. The title has a meaning of 'understanding other players' mind'.

[2] '制心' means 'to control the mind'. Therefore, this 'mind' indicates the player's own mind. For '收其放心', read reference: 宋司马光的《答景仁论养生及乐书》，"朝夕出入起居，未尝不在礼乐之间，以收其放心，检其慢志，此礼乐之所以为用也"。

贵和章第三十	**Rule 30. Treasuring friendships**
君子无所争，（正己而不求于人。）	**Worthy people have nothing to prove,** [1] (They are able to promote self-cultivation by themselves, without asking others to do anything.)
和而不同。（捶丸处，虽若平等相近，而尊卑之序不可紊乱。）	**Develop a good friendship, but maintain individual players' personalities.** (Although all players are equal in *chui wan* game, their different social hierarchies must not be disordered.) [2]
奴颜巧言，佞也；（就场论是谈非，称长道短，巧佞之人，不可近也。）	**Being servile and ingratiate themselves, These people are flatterers.** (In the playing field, some players gossip and make irresponsible remarks. These are sycophants, with whom you should not associate.)
正虑随情，和也。（但思捶击之法，自为娱乐，无有争也。）	**If the players can keep their concentration on what should be done and play with a pleasant manner, the game will be harmonious.** (If the players only think about the techniques of *chui wan* and try to entertain themselves, there will be nothing to fight over.)
和而不同，君子贵之。（贵贱有等，不相夷躐，成德者贵重之。）	**Pursuing harmonious relations and maintaining differences of personal charactors in between the players. are what honourable people value.** (Noblemen and humble men are in a ranking order and the ranking cannot be levelled or overstepped. Moral people highly value this.)
便佞取赢，君子不贵也。（便僻巧佞，务取胜于人者，君子不与也。）	**Some players act servilely with overpraising in order to win. Honourable people do not appreciate this.** (Honourable people should avoid the people who endeavour to win with sweet-words and sycophancy.)

[1] See 《论语·八佾》: Honorable people have nothing to fight for. If must have one, then take archery competition as an example, contestants must follow the rule of competition etiquette for archery competition, which are: greet to each other with courtesy before playing, e.g. to bow each other, and drink together after the competition. This is the competition of honorable people, which is contest about the etiquette.
[2] The original text says keeping differences from each other. It does not specially indicate social hierarchy.

待傲章第三十一	**Rule 31. Dealing with haughty behaviours**
以多待一曰傲，（众待其来，其人慢期不至，傲也。）	**Many people are held up because one player is late. The late person should be described as haughty.** (Many players await this player to come, but he is late for a long time. This is a haughty behaviour.)
众不悦一曰孤，（所作不可人意，自逞其能，孤也。）	**If many people are unhappy with one player's hehaviour, that person will be isolated.** (The player's behaviour is not acceptable by others, and that player presumes his capability is so high that he can ignore others' feeling. He is solitary.)
轻佻曰贱，（行止轻薄，故曰贱人。）	**Frivolous behaviours can be regarded as being unpleasant.** (If player's behaviour is frivolous, he may be called an unpleasant person.)

取恶曰凶。（所为侵犯于人，人疾恶之，故曰凶人。）	**Malicious actions are ferocious.** (If a player's behaviour is harmful to others, he will be extremely hated by others. Therefore, he should be called a scoundrel.)
跛足、目盲、伛偻、耳聋，不可与也。（残疾者，不与嬉乐。）	**People who are lame, blind, hunch or deaf cannot join the game.** (Do not play the game for fun with disabled people.)
便佞之徒，不足道也。（谄曲之人，不足与言。便，平声。）	**It is not worth talking to flatterers.** (To people who like to flatter others, it is not worth talking to them.)
是故贵贱不相效，（贱者不敢效贵，效则干犯在上之人而取败矣。）	**Consequently, people with different levels of morality do not learn from each other.** (Menial people dare not to imitate noble people. If they do, they can be accused of offending their superiors, which means they will get a result of losing the game.) [1]
同类必相求。（朋友之交可以相效。）	**People of same types are certainly free to ask one another for help,** (Among good friends, people can imitate each other.)
多胜无矜色，数败无恚容，君子也。（多胜不夸，数败无怒，君子也。）	**Worthy players will not show conceit or haughtiness after many victories, nor anger and annoyance after repeated failures.** (A worthy player will not praise himself even after many wins and not become angry following a number of losses.)

[1] The original text mentions '贵贱', noble people and menial people，who do not learn from each other. It is not only said that menial people do not imitate noble people. The effect of this imitation on the games is not mentioned. Here and in the whole original text, '贵贱'(noble and menial people) seem to depends on people's morality, rather than their family backgrounds or wealth.

知人章第三十二	**Rule 32. Knowing your fellow players**
观志知人，（观其意趣，可知人之善恶。）	**Recognising person's aspirations allows you to know him.** (Looking at a person's desires and interests, you can know him on both good side and bad side.)
观心知己。（内观此心，则己之言行，亦可自知也。）	**Examining your own mind allows you to know yourself.** (Looking at what you think, you can understand whether what you are saying and what you are doing are appropriate.)
心欲宁，（心要静定。）	**Your mind likes to be peaceful.** (Your mind should be calm and relaxed.)
志欲逸，（志欲宁适。）	**Your aspirations and interests like to be appropriate.** (Your aspirations should be tranquil and appropriate.)
气欲平，（气要温和。）	**'Qi' in your body intends to be steady.** (The movement of 'qi ' in your body should be gentle and mild.) [1]

体欲安，（体要安舒。）	**Your body likes to be in a peaceful state.** (You should physically feel relaxed and comfortable.)
貌欲恭，（容止端庄。）	**Your facial expression should show respect to others.** (Your facial expression should be dignified.)
言欲讷。（语言简当。）	**Your style of conversation like to be short and slow.** (Your speech should be simple and appropriate.)
有诸中必形诸外，（由乎中应乎外。）	**The inner characters in your mind will inevitably show in your outer appearance.** (Your appearance reflects what you have in your mind.)
胜负决矣，（捶丸胜负已定。）	**When the result of the game has been determined,** (The winning or losing of *chui wan* has been decided.)
正赛行矣。（赌赛已毕。）	**The competition ends.** (The gambling is over.)
体不安，（观其手足失措。）	**If a player seems to be restless,** (You can see that his hands and feet are uncoordinated.)
貌不恭，（容止急躁。）	**his facial expression shows disrespect,** (his face shows an impatient expression.)
作于意，（意思嗔恚。）	**his actions reflect his indignant feeling,** (he is angry.)
见于色，（颜色愠怒。）	**his anger becomes visible on his face,** (There is a resentful look on his face.)
形于言，（出言不让。）	**his words indicate his fury,** (His conversation becomes strident.)
小人也。（此等可见其为小人也。）	**this is an unworthy man.** (All these indicate that he is clearly an unworthy man.)
心平气和，不形于色，不作于意，君子也。（胜负不动于心，容止自若，成德人也。）	**Calm and peaceful, not showing your mind on your face, not act like an angry man, these are what worthy people should do.** (No matter winning or losing the game, your mind is not disturbed, your facial expression and behaviour are well controlled. This is the way to be a respected person.)

[1] *'Qi'* is a term used in traditional Chinese medicine. It is an invisible fluid delivering energy to all parts of a body.

破式次之達式出之

體面折旋中矩閑旋

[若喜怒見面列口傷

諫人先拋趣兒得采

Made in the USA
Charleston, SC
22 December 2016